**G. SCHIRMER
COLLECTION
OPERA LIBRETTOS**

DAS RHEINGOLD
Prologue to the Trilogy DER RING DES NIBELUNGEN
In One Act

by
Richard Wagner

English Version by
STEWART ROBB

Ed. 2774

G. SCHIRMER, Inc.

Important Notice

Performances of this opera must be licensed by the publisher.

All rights of any kind with respect to this opera and any parts thereof, including but not limited to stage, radio, television, motion picture, mechanical reproduction, translation, printing, and selling are strictly reserved.

License to perform this work, in whole or in part, whether with instrumental or keyboard accompaniment, must be secured in writing from the Publisher. Terms will be quoted upon request.

Copying of either separate parts or the whole of this work, by hand or by any other process, is unlawful and punishable under the provisions of the U.S.A. Copyright Act.

The use of any copies, including arrangements and orchestrations, other than those issued by the Publisher, is forbidden.

All inquiries should be directed to the Publisher:

G. Schirmer Rental Department
5 Bellvale Road
Chester, NY 10918
(914) 469-2271

Copyright © 1960 (Renewed) by Stewart Robb
Sole Selling Agent: G. Schirmer, Inc.
International Copyright Secured. All Rights Reserved.
**Warning: Unauthorized reproduction of this publication is
prohibited by Federal law and subject to criminal prosecution.**

DAS RHEINGOLD

Everything about Richard Wagner's *Ring des Nibelungen* is cut to gigantic size. One unified musico-dramatic concept, it takes over seventeen hours to perform, demands artists with unusual physical stamina and great histrionic ability and requires audience attention for four long theatrical evenings. Not least of its large-scale ideas is its prologue. Instead of the conventional aria before the curtain as in *Pagliacci,* Wagner's prologue, *Das Rheingold,* stretches for two-and-a-half hours of unbroken music. Yet for all of its great size, the *Ring* or any of its parts succeeds through individual incidents and characterizations that make the whole drama a human epic.

Das Rheingold was the last *Ring* libretto to be written and the first music to be composed. After Wagner, then Kapellmeister in Dresden, completed *Lohengrin* in 1848, he involved himself on the losing side of a local revolution. Banished from Saxony and living in Switzerland, he developed the concept of his music drama, in which words and music would be combined to such an equal degree that neither would be more important than the other. As a vehicle for his new concept, the complete art work, the German epic *Das Nibelungenlied,* which descends from the *Edda* in Scandinavian lore, appealed to him. First, the composer sketched a poem, *Siegfrieds Tod (Siegfried's Death)*. From 1848 to 1853 he worked from his first poem, explaining backwards in the saga until his four books of *Der Ring des Nibelungen* told the ancient legend in Wagnerian terms. But what does it all mean? Over the years, theories of nationalism, socialism, Freudian psychiatry, Jungian metaphysics have all been tried without any theory really explaining everything in the *Ring*. The theory that stands up best is the simplest: Wagner knew how to spin a good story, loved to work in the domain of otherworldly and larger-than-life characters and made basic German mythology express the important themes of his life.

These themes — the defeat of greed, redemption of the world by a woman's selfless love, the need to follow one's own destiny and the inability to predict successfully one's future — appear in every *Ring* opera, including *Das Rheingold*. But here their expression is cryptic. The composer uses his prologue to set out the subject matter of the whole drama and to give it its musical basis as well without allowing time for emotional expansion on any one point. In its brevity and tautness, Wagner's meshing of music and story here reaches its zenith — no extraneous words, no extreme emotions. But the triumph of theory has made *Das Rheingold* the *Ring's* least popular opera. The composer says what he wants to say so quickly that the audience hardly has time to respond or to identify with the characters. Yet the work does not fail. It simply demands a greater unity of purpose and breadth of understanding on the part of performers, conductor, producer and director to make its jewels shine with the radiance of the later *Ring* operas.

In the world of the *Ring,* there are three strata. In the caves under the earth dwell the Nibelungs, dwarfs who mine the precious elements out of base rock. On the earth live the giants, huge, muscular and rather slow-witted creatures. In the heavens dwell the gods. Each god (and this is particularly characteristic of Germanic mythology) is associated with the seasons or the climactic elements. The gods are themselves controlled by the fates but have power of life and death over man. Humans live on earth, as do the giants, but do not have major roles to fill at the point in time of *Das Rheingold*. Though the three divisions of the world are not at war with one another when the drama opens, their conflict is inevitable.

The continuity of the *Ring* cycle comes from the many leitmotivs (more than eighty in *Das Rheingold* alone). These musical signature tunes represent characters, things and states of mind of individual characters; in this first drama of the *Ring,* they appear in their most uncomplicated form. But continuity in Western culture comes from nature, and the *Ring* opens in the depths of the river Rhine. The E-flat major triad that paints the river's inexorable flow prepares the audience for entertainment on a titanic scale. This feeling of primitive consciousness gave Wagner the impetus to put pen to paper and begin the cycle's music. For months he had wrestled with how to begin his great work. On a trip to Italy in autumn 1853, he found himself in a hotel at Spezia on the Italian seacoast. Half-sick with nerves and dysentery, he threw himself on a hard couch and fell into a restless sleep. Suddenly, green water seemed to envelop him and the pure triad of E-flat major surged from the recesses of his brain. *Das Rheingold* had begun.

He started serious composition on November 1, 1853, finishing it on January 14. Orchestration occupied him until May 28 when the prologue was finished. The first performance took place in Munich at the Hof-und-National Theater, on September 22, 1869. King Ludwig, Wagner's royal protector, had waited many years to hear the *Ring*. Though Wagner did not want to have any of the operas performed until all were ready, the King ordered *Rheingold* into performance. From the beginning, the technical side of the *Ring* offered seemingly insurmountable problems; for this first performance, Wagner's attempt to pull the strings while not in Munich constantly confused everything. The opera was not successfully received, but when performed at the first Bayreuth Festival (August 13, 1876) came into its own. For that first Bayreuth performance, under the leadership of Hans Richter, Franz Betz was Wotan, Karl Hill, Alberich and Heinrich Vogl, Loge. The opera was first performed in America at the Metropolitan Opera House on January 4, 1889, with Emil Fischer (Wotan), Joseph Bech (Alberich) and Max Alvary (Loge), under the baton of Anton Seidl. The production of *Das Rheingold*, unveiled on November 22, 1968, with staging by conductor Herbert von Karajan and sets by Günther Schneider-Siemssen, marks the work's fourth mounting at the Metropolitan Opera.

SPEIGHT JENKINS, JR.

THE STORY

In the murky depths of the river Rhine swim three mermaids, Woglinde, Wellgunde and Flosshilde, keeping guard over the precious Rhinegold. The dwarf Alberich interrupts their play; stirred by the girls' beauty, he tries to catch them, but they manage to elude his grasp while mocking him with words of endearment. Suddenly a sunbeam illuminates the Rhinegold, which the maidens hail, rashly revealing that the one who renounces love and makes a ring from the gold can become master of the universe. Alberich, frustrated in his attempts to win love, curses its power; climbing the rock as the Rhinemaidens cry out in alarm, he seizes the treasure and disappears.

On a lofty mountain top, Fricka awakens her husband, Wotan, the father of gods and men. As he rises, Wotan is transfixed by the sight of the gods' newly completed home, Valhalla, in the heavens. Fricka chides him for having offered Freia, goddess of love and youth, to the giants Fafner and Fasolt as payment for their labors in building the stronghold. Just as Wotan reassures her that he will not live up to this bargain, the terrified Freia, pursued by the giants, rushes in calling on her brothers Donner and Froh for protection. After hearing Fasolt's demands, Wotan stalls for time by consulting with the crafty god of fire, Loge, who has also joined them. Loge scores the deities on their ingratitude for his efforts in searching the world for a worthy payment to replace Freia; he has found but one possible substitute — Alberich's all-powerful gold. When the giants show interest, Loge suggests robbing the dwarf. Accepting the plan, the giants carry off Freia as hostage until Wotan can deliver the new payment in full. Deprived of the goddess of youth, the gods begin to age. At length Wotan, fearing for their lives, descends with Loge into the earth to wrest the gold from Alberich.

In a cavern deep beneath the earth in the realm of the enslaved Nibelungs, Alberich gloats over his riches and power. Tormenting his brother Mime, Alberich demonstrates the magic of the Tarnhelm, a helmet of chain-mail that makes the wearer invisible. When Wotan and Loge appear, Mime whiningly describes how his brother fashioned the Rhinegold into a ring. Suddenly Alberich returns, driving a group of howling Nibelungs before him with a whip. Wotan tells the dwarf that he and Loge have come to witness a show of his fabled powers. Through the magic of the Tarnhelm, Alberich turns himself into a giant serpent; when he takes the shape of a toad, however, Wotan puts his foot on the helpless creature while Loge snatches the helmet from its head. Alberich resumes his own shape, whereupon the gods bind and drag him off.

Back at the earth's surface, Wotan exacts from Alberich as the price of his freedom all of the hoard — carried in by the pitiful Nibelungs — the Tarnhelm and last the Ring itself, which he rips from the reluctant dwarf's finger. Alberich calls down a curse upon the Ring and all who shall possess it. The dwarf disappears into the mist; both gods and giants return. As Freia's ransom, Fafner and Fasolt stipulate that she must be hidden from their sight by the gold. When the entire treasure is piled high, Fasolt finds a chink through which the goddess' eyes are still visible, and demands that it be filled with the ring on Wotan's finger. Wotan's refusal brings forth the earth goddess Erda, who rises from her sleepy bed to prophesy the gods' doom if the Ring remains in their hands. At this, Wotan relents. No sooner is Freia freed than the giants quarrel over dividing their riches; Fafner kills Fasolt and hurries off with the gold, while Wotan muses on the power of Alberich's curse. The mists that have obscured Valhalla from sight are dispersed by Donner with his thunderbolts. As the castle appears at the end of a shimmering rainbow bridge, Wotan hails his magnificent home, bathed in a sunset glow, toward which the gods now proceed. Only Loge lingers to remark that they are hurrying to their doom. From the valley below, the Rhinemaidens are heard lamenting their lost treasure; though Wotan bids Loge silence them, their cries persist as the gods make their entry into Valhalla.

Courtesy Opera News

CAST OF CHARACTERS

WOGLINDE		Soprano
WELLGUNDE	*Rhinemaidens*	Mezzo-Soprano
FLOSSHILDE		Mezzo-Soprano
ALBERICH, a Nibelung dwarf		Baritone
FRICKA, queen of the gods		Mezzo-Soprano
WOTAN, king of the gods		Baritone
FREIA, goddess of youth and love		Soprano
FASOLT	*Giants*	Bass
FAFNER		Bass
FROH, god of the fields		Tenor
DONNER, god of thunder		Baritone
LOGE, god of fire		Tenor
MIME, Alberich's brother		Tenor
ERDA, goddess of the earth		Contralto

SYNOPSIS OF SCENES

		Page
SCENE 1.	The bed of the river Rhine	1
SCENE 2.	A mountain top above the Rhine valley	6
SCENE 3.	The caverns of Nibelhome	14
SCENE 4.	A mountain top above the Rhine valley	20

DAS RHEINGOLD

1. Szene

Auf dem Grund des Rheines

Grünliche Dämmerung, nach oben zu lichter, nach unten zu dunkler. Die Höhe ist von wogendem Gewässer erfüllt, das rastlos von rechts nach links zu strömt. Nach der Tiefe zu lösen sich die Fluten in einen immer feineren feuchten Nebe auf, so daß der Raum der Manneshöhe vom Boden auf gänzlich frei vom Wasser zu sein scheint, welches wie in Wolkenzügen über den nächtlichen Grund dahinfließt. Überall ragen schroffe Felsenriffe aus der Tiefe auf und grenzen den Raum der Bühne ab; der ganze Boden ist in ein wildes Zackengewirr zerspalten, so daß er nirgends vollkommen eben ist und nach allen Seiten hin in dichtester Finsternis tiefere Schluchten annehmen läßt.

Um ein Riff in der Mitte der Bühne, welches mit seiner schlanken Spitze bis in die dichtere, heller dämmernde Wasserflut hinaufragt, kreist in anmutig schwimmender Bewegung eine der Rheintöchter.

WOGLINDE

Weia! Waga!
Woge, du Welle,
walle zur Wiege!
Wagala weia!
Wallala, weiala weia!

WELLGUNDE
(Stimme, von oben)

Woglinde, wachst du allein?

WOGLINDE

Mit Wellgunde wär' ich zu zwei.
(taucht aus der Flut zum Riff herab)

WELLGUNDE

Lass' seh'n, wie du wachst.

WOGLINDE
(entweicht ihr schwimmend)

Sicher vor dir.
(Sie necken sich und suchen sich spielend zu fangen.)

FLOSSHILDE
(Stimme, von oben)

Heiaha weia!
Wildes Geschwister!

WELLGUNDE

Flosshilde, schwimm'!
Woglinde flieht:
hilf mir die Fliessende fangen!

FLOSSHILDE
(taucht herab und fährt zwischen die Spielenden)

Des Goldes Schlaf
hütet ihr schlecht!
Besser bewacht
des Schlummernden Bett,
sonst büsst ihr beide das Spiel!

(Mit muntrem Gekreisch fahren die beiden auseinander: Floßhilde sucht bald die eine, bald die andere zu erhaschen; sie entschlüpfen ihr und vereinigen sich endlich, um gemeinschaftlich auf Floßhilde Jagd zu machen; so schnellen sie gleich Fischen von Riff zu Riff, scherzend und lachend.)

Aus einer finsteren Schlucht ist währenddem Alberich, an einem Riffe klimmend, dem Abgrunde entstiegen. Er hält, noch vom Dunkel umgeben, an und schaut dem Spiele der Wassermädchen mit steigendem Wohlgefallen zu.

ALBERICH

Hehe! Ihr Nicker!
Wie seid ihr niedlich,
neidliches Volk!
Aus Nibelheims Nacht
naht' ich mich gern,
neigtet ihr euch zu mir.

(Die Mädchen halten, als sie Alberichs Stimme hören, mit ihrem Spiele ein.)

WOGLINDE

Hei! wer ist dort?

FLOSSHILDE

Es dämmert und ruft.

WELLGUNDE

Lugt, wer uns belauscht!
(Sie tauchen tiefer herab und erkennen den Nibelung.)

WOGLINDE, WELLGUNDE

Pfui! der Garstige!

FLOSSHILDE
(schnell auftauchend)

Hütet das Gold!
(Die beiden andern folgen ihr, und alle drei versammeln sich schnell um das mittlere Riff.)
Vater warnte
vor solchem Feind.

THE RHINEGOLD

Scene 1

At the Bottom of the Rhine

Greenish twilight, lighter above, darker below. The upper part of the scene is filled with moving water. Toward the ground the waters distill into a fine mist which flows like a train of clouds over the gloomy depths. Everywhere steep points of rock jut up, while the ground is a confusion of jagged pieces, with no place level.
Round a rock into whose peak rises the lighter water, a Rhine-nymph is seen swimming.

VOGLINDA

Weia! Waga!
Lull us, you waters,
cradle and rock us!
Wagalaweia!
Wallala weiala weia!

VELLGUNDA'S VOICE
(from above)
Voglinda, are you on guard?

VOGLINDA

Alone, till our Vellgunda comes.
(diving from the surface to the reef)

VELLGUNDA

Let's see how you watch.

VOGLINDA
(avoiding her by swimming)
Out of your reach!
(They seek playfully to catch each other.)

FLOSSHILDA'S VOICE
(from above)
Heiala weia!
Hey, you wild sisters!

VELLGUNDA

Flosshilda, swim!
Voglinda flees!
Help me to capture our sister!

FLOSSHILDA
(diving down)
You guard the gold
badly today!
Watch with more care
the slumberer's bed,
else both will pay for your play!

(The two separate with merry cries. Flosshilda chases first one, then the other. They evade her, then unite to pursue her in turn. Darting about like fish from rock to rock they laugh and sport.

From a dark chasm Alberich clambers up to one of the rocks. He halts in a shadow and watches the nymphs with increasing delight.)

ALBERICH

Ho, ho, you nixies!
What an enchanting,
delicate folk!
From Nibelhome's night
welcome a guest
who'd like to come near.
(The girls leave off playing.)

VOGLINDA

Hey! who is there?

FLOSSHILDA

It's dark and it speaks!

VOGLINDA

Look out for the spy!
(They dive down deeper to perceive the Nibelung.)

VOGLINDA & VELLGUNDA

Pfui! a nasty imp!

FLOSSHILDA
(darting upward)
Look to the gold!
(The others follow her, and all three quickly gather round the central rock.)
Father warned us
of such a foe.

1

Alberich
Ihr, da oben!

Die drei Rheintöchter
Was willst du dort unten?

Alberich
Stör' ich eu'r Spiel,
wenn staunend ich still hier steh'?
Tauchtet ihr nieder,
mit euch tollte
und neckte der Niblung sich gern.

Woglinde
Mit uns will er spielen?

Wellgunde
Ist ihm das Spott?

Alberich
Wie scheint im Schimmer
ihr hell und schön!
Wie gern umschlänge
der Schlanken eine mein Arm,
schlüpfte hold sie herab!

Flosshilde
Nun lach' ich der Furcht:
der Feind ist verliebt.
(Sie lachen.)

Wellgunde
Der lüsterne Kauz!

Woglinde
Lasst ihn uns kennen!
(Sie läßt sich auf die Spitze des Riffes hinab, an dessen Fuße Alberich angelangt ist.)

Alberich
Die neigt sich herab.

Woglinde
Nun nahe dich mir!

Alberich
(klettert mit koboldartiger Behendigkeit, doch wiederholt aufgehalten, der Spitze des Riffes zu)
Garstig glatter
glitschriger Glimmer!
Wie gleit' ich aus!
Mit Händen und Füssen
nicht fasse noch halt' ich
das schlecke Geschlüpfer!
Feuchtes Nass
füllt mir die Nase:
verfluchtes Niessen!
(Er ist in Woglindes Nähe angelangt.)

Woglinde
(lachend)
Prustend naht
meines Freiers Pracht!

Alberich
(Er sucht sie zu umfassen.)
Mein Friedel sei,
du fräuliches Kind!

Woglinde
(sich ihm entwindend)
Willst du mich frei'n,
so freie mich hier!

Alberich
(kratzt sich den Kopf)
O weh! du entweichst?
Komm' doch wieder!
Schwer ward mir,
was so leicht du erschwingst.

Woglinde
(schwingt sich auf ein drittes Riff in größerer Tiefe)
Steig' nur zu Grund:
da greifst du mich sicher!

Alberich
Wohl besser da unten!

Woglinde
(schnellt sich rasch aufwärts nach einem hohen Seitenriffe)
Nun aber nach oben!

Wellgunde, Flosshilde
Ha ha ha ha ha ha!

Alberich
Wie fang' ich im Sprung
den spröden Fisch?
(Er will ihr eilig nachklettern.)
Warte, du Falsche!

Wellgunde
(hat sich auf ein tieferes Riff auf der andern Seite gesenkt)
Heia! Du Holder!
hörst du mich nicht?

Alberich
(sich umwendend)
Rufst du nach mir?

Wellgunde
Ich rate dir wohl:
zu mir wende dich,
Woglinde meide!

ALBERICH
Hey, you up there!

THE THREE GIRLS
What's up with you, down there?

ALBERICH
Would I disturb your play
if I stood and watched?
Dive to me downward.
This poor Nibelung
would love to be romping with you!

VOGLINDA
He wishes to join us?

VELLGUNDA
Surely he jokes?

ALBERICH
How fair and bright
in the light you seem!
I'd like to put my arm
round your delicate waist—
if you'd kindly come down!

FLOSSHILDA
My fear has all gone!
The foe is in love!
(They laugh.)

VELLGUNDA
Lascivious owl!

VOGLINDA
Let us approach him!
(She lets herself to the peak of the rock, at the foot of which Alberich is.)

ALBERICH
She's coming down here!

VOGLINDA
Now try to come near.

ALBERICH
(clambers with gnomelike nimbleness, but with difficulty, to the point of the rock)
What a slimy,
slippery surface!
I slide and slip!
My hands and my feet
cannot find any place
that is good to support me.
Muggy dampness
fills up my nostrils.
(Sneezes.)
Accursed sneezing!
(He has approached Voglinda.)

VOGLINDA
(laughing)
See how finely
my love can sneeze!

ALBERICH
(trying to clasp her)
O, be my dear,
you womanly child!

VOGLINDA
(eluding him)
If you would woo,
then woo me up here!

ALBERICH
(scratching his head)
Alas! You don't stay!
Come once more here!
Hard for me—
what is easy for you.

VOGLINDA
(swinging down to a third rock in the depths)
Clamber down here,
then grip me quite firmly.

ALBERICH
Much better down lower.
(She darts up to a rock at the side.)

VOGLINDA
But now I am higher!
(The nymphs all laugh.)

ALBERICH
Just how shall I catch
this scary fish?
(He hastily clambers after her.)
Wait a bit, false one!

VELLGUNDA
(has descended to a low rock on the opposite side)
Heia, my fine one!
Can you not hear?

ALBERICH
(turning around)
O, did you call?

VELLGUNDA
I caution you well,
just come here to me:
keep from Voglinda!

ALBERICH
(klettert hastig über den Bodengrund zu Wellgunde)

Viel schöner bist du
als jene Scheue,
die minder gleissend
und gar zu glatt. —
Nur tiefer tauche,
willst du mir taugen!

WELLGUNDE
(noch etwas mehr zu ihm sich herabsenkend)

Bin nun ich dir nah?

ALBERICH

Noch nicht genug!
Die schlanken Arme
schlinge um mich,
dass ich den Nacken
dir neckend betaste,
mit schmeichelnder Brunst
an die schwellende Brust mich dir schmiege!

WELLGUNDE

Bist du verliebt
und lüstern nach Minne?
lass' seh'n, du Schöner,
wie bist du zu schau'n? —
Pfui! du haariger,
höckriger Geck!
Schwarzes, schwieliges
Schwefelgezwerg!
(Er sucht sie mit Gewalt zu halten)
Such' dir ein Friedel,
dem du gefällst!

ALBERICH

Gefall' ich dir nicht,
dich fass' ich doch fest!

WELLGUNDE
(schnell zum mittleren Riffe auftauchend)

Nur fest, sonst fliess' ich dir fort!

WOGLINDE, FLOSSHILDE

Ha ha ha ha ha ha!

ALBERICH
(Wellgunde erbost nachzankend)

Falsches Kind!
Kalter, grätiger Fisch!
Schein' ich nicht schön dir,
niedlich und neckisch,
glatt und glau, —
hei! so buhle mit Aalen,
ist dir eklig mein Balg!

FLOSSHILDE

Was zankst du, Alp?
Schon so verzagt?
Du freitest um zwei:
frügst du die dritte,
süssen Trost
schüfe die Traute dir!

ALBERICH

Holder Sang
singt zu mir her.
Wie gut, dass ihr
eine nicht seid!
Von vielen gefall' ich wohl einer:
bei einer kieste mich keine! —
Soll ich dir glauben,
so gleite herab!

FLOSSHILDE
(taucht zu Alberich hinab)

Wie törig seid ihr,
dumme Schwestern,
dünkt euch dieser nicht schön!

ALBERICH
(ihr nahend)

Für dumm und hässlich
darf ich sie halten,
seit ich dich Holdeste seh'.

FLOSSHILDE

O singe fort
so süss und fein;
wie hehr verführt es mein Ohr!

ALBERICH
(zutraulich sie berührend)

Mir zagt, zuckt
und zehrt sich das Herz,
lacht mir so zierliches Lob.

FLOSSHILDE

Wie deine Anmut
mein Aug' erfreut,
deines Lächelns Milde
den Mut mir labt!
(Sie zieht ihn zärtlich an sich.)
Seligster Mann!

THE RHINEGOLD

ALBERICH
(while he hastily clambers over the rocky ground toward Vellgunda.)

You're fairer far
than that one who's shy.
Her form's less shining,
and much too smooth.
Just dive down deeper,
if you would reach me.

VELLGUNDA
(descending a little)

So now am I near?

ALBERICH

Not yet enough!
Just twine your slender arms
about me,
that I may fondle
your neck with my fingers,
and tenderly, ardently,
press myself close to your bosom!

VELLGUNDA

Are you in love,
and pining for kindness?
Let's see, you beauty,
just what you can show!
Pfui! you hunchbacked,
horrible gawk!
Swarthy, scurvy
and sulphurous dwarf!
(Alberich tries to detain her by force.)
Look for a sweetheart
like to yourself!

ALBERICH

Although I'm not cute,
I'll capture you fast!

VELLGUNDA
(darting up to the central rock)

Quite fast,
or else I'll be gone.

VOGLINDA & FLOSSHILDA
(laughing)

Ha ha ha ha ha ha!

ALBERICH
(calling angrily after Vellgunda)

Lying child!
Bony, frostbitten fish!
Am I not lovely,
dainty and pleasant,
smooth and bright!
Get eels for your lovers,
if you find my skin foul!

FLOSSHILDA

Why scold so, imp?
Why be cast down?
You've wooed only two—
ask now the third one:
one quite sweet
promises sweet reward!

ALBERICH

That's a song
good for my ears!
How fine to find
more than just one.
I think I'll please one out of many—
with one though, none of them wants me!
Let me believe you:
so come here below!

FLOSSHILDA
(dives down to Alberich)

How foolish are
my stupid sisters
not to find you quite fair!

ALBERICH
(approaching her hastily)

How dull and base
seems all that they are,
compared to the charms that are yours.

FLOSSHILDA

O, sing right on
in gentle tone;
your voice seduces my ears!

ALBERICH
(touching her caressingly)

I shake, thrill,
and flutter at heart,
hearing your honey-sweet praise.

FLOSSHILDA

How your attractiveness
joys my eyes!
With your gentle smile
you inspire my soul!
(drawing him tenderly to her)
Blessedest man!

ALBERICH
Süsseste Maid!

FLOSSHILDE
Wär'st du mir hold!

ALBERICH
Hielt' ich dich immer!

FLOSSHILDE
Deinen stechenden Blick,
deinen struppigen Bart,
o säh' ich ihn, fasst' ich ihn stets!
Deines stachlichen Haares
strammes Gelock,
umflöss' es Flosshilde ewig!
Deine Krötengestalt,
deiner Stimme Gekrächz,
o dürft' ich, staunend und stumm,
sie nur hören und seh'n!

WOGLINDE, WELLGUNDE
Ha ha ha ha ha ha!

ALBERICH
(erschreckt aus Floßhildes Armen auffahrend)
Lacht ihr Bösen mich aus?

FLOSSHILDE
(sich plötzlich ihm entreißend)
Wie billig am Ende vom Lied.
(Sie taucht mit den Schwestern schnell auf.)

WOGLINDE, WELLGUNDE
Ha ha ha ha ha ha!

ALBERICH
(mit kreischender Stimme)
Wehe! ach wehe!
O Schmerz! O Schmerz!
Die dritte, so traut,
betrog sie mich auch? —
Ihr schmählich schlaues,
lüderlich schlechtes Gelichter!
Nährt ihr nur Trug,
ihr treuloses Nickergezücht?

DIE DREI RHEINTÖCHTER
Wallala! Wallala! Lalaleia!
Leialalei! Heia! Heia! Ha ha!
Schäme dich, Albe!
Schilt nicht dort unten!
Höre, was wir dich heissen!
Warum, du Banger,
bandest du nicht
das Mädchen, das du minnst?
Treu sind wir
und ohne Trug
dem Freier, der uns fängt. —
Greife nur zu,
und grause dich nicht!
In der Flut entflieh'n wir nicht leicht.
Wallala! Lalaleia! Leialalei!
Heia! Heia! Ha hei!
(Sie schwimmen auseinander, hierher und dorthin, bald tiefer, bald höher, um Alberich zur Jagd auf sie zu reizen.)

ALBERICH
Wie in den Gliedern
brünstige Glut
mir brennt und glüht!
Wut und Minne,
wild und mächtig,
wühlt mir den Mut auf. —
Wie ihr auch lacht und lügt,
lüstern lechz' ich nach euch,
und eine muss mir erliegen!

(Er macht sich mit verzweifelter Anstrengung zur Jagd auf; mit grauenhafter Behendigkeit erklimmt er Riff für Riff, springt von einem zum andern, sucht bald dieses, bald jenes der Mädchen zu erhaschen, die mit lustigem Gekreisch stets ihm entweichen; er strauchelt, stürzt in den Abgrund hinab, klettert dann hastig wieder in die Höhe zu neuer Jagd. Sie neigen sich etwas herab. Fast erreicht er sie, stürzt abermals zurück und versucht es nochmals Er hält endlich vor Wut schäumend atemlos an und streckt die geballte Faust nach den Mädchen hinauf.)

Fing' eine diese Faust!...

(Er verbleibt in sprachloser Wut, den Blick aufwärts gerichtet, wo er dann plötzlich von folgendem Schauspiele angezogen und gefesselt wird. — Durch die Flut ist von oben her ein immer lichterer Schein gedrungen, der sich an einer hohen Stelle des mitelsten Riffes allmählich zu einem blendend hell strahlenden Goldglanze entzündet, ein zauberisch goldenes Licht bricht von hier durch das Wasser.)

WOGLINDE
Lugt, Schwestern!
Die Weckerin lacht in den Grund.

WELLGUNDE
Durch den grünen Schwall
den wonnigen Schläfer sie grüsst.

FLOSSHILDE
Jetzt küsst sie sein Auge,
dass er es öffne.

WELLGUNDE
Schaut, er lächelt
in lichtem Schein.

WOGLINDE
Durch die Fluten hin
fliesst sein strahlender Stern!

DIE DREI RHEINTÖCHTER
Heiajaheia! Heiajaheia!
Wallala la la la leia jahei!
Rheingold! Rheingold!

ALBERICH
Sweetest of maids!

FLOSSHILDA
Were you but mine!

ALBERICH
Be mine for ever!

FLOSSHILDA
O! your piercing old glance,
and your bristly old beard,
to see them and feel them forever!
That your flourishing locks
of porcupine hair
might float round Flosshilda always!
With your form like a toad,
and your voice like a croak,
O, might I, mute and amazed,
only see and hear these!

VOGLINDA & VELLGUNDA
Ha ha ha ha ha ha!

ALBERICH
(timidly)
Are you laughing at me?

FLOSSHILDA
(suddenly tearing herself from him)
How fitting an end to the song!
(She darts up to her sisters and joins them in their laughter.)

ALBERICH
(with screaming voice)
Woe's me! Ah, woe's me!
Alas! Alas!
The third one, so dear,
betrays me as well?
You shocking, wily,
wicked, disorderly riff-raff!
Brood of the nixies,
treacherous breeders of lies!

VOGLINDA, VELLGUNDA & FLOSSHILDA

Walala! Lalaleia! Lalei!
Heiaha! Heia! Haha!
Shame on you, elf-man,
scolding down yonder!
Take the counsel we tender!
Just why, you faint-heart,
did you not tie
the lady that you love?
True are we,
free of deceit
to wooers when we're caught.
Capture us, then,
and have no more fear,
for our speed is slow in the waves.
(They swim about, hither and thither, high and low, to incite Alberich to pursuit.)

ALBERICH
Right through my limbs
there rages a fire
which burns and glows!
Wrath and ardor,
wild and mighty,
rake up my spirit!
Though you may laugh and lie,
passion urges me on,
And one must yield to my lusting.
(He pursues them with desperate efforts, clambering from rock to rock, springing from one to another, and striving to reach first one nymph and then another, while they always escape him with merry cries. He staggers, falls below, and then climbs up hastily again, undaunted. They descend a little lower. At last, his patience exhausted, he pauses breathless and shakes his fist at them.)
One only in my grip!
(He remains in speechless rage gazing upward, when suddenly he is riveted to the spot, for through the water above breaks an ever-increasing glow, which on the summit of the central rock kindles gradually to a blinding yellow gleam; a magical golden light then streams from thence through the water.)

VOGLINDA
Look, sisters!
The wakener laughs in the deep.

VELLGUNDA
Through dark green surge
he calls the blest sleeper to wake.

FLOSSHILDA
He kisses her eyelids,
so they will open.

VELLGUNDA
See her smiling
with gentle light!

VOGLINDA
Through the darkling waves
shines our radiant star!

ALL THREE GIRLS
Heiajaheia!
Heiajaheia!
Walalalalaleia jahei!
Rhinegold!

Leuchtende Lust,
wie lachst du so hell und hehr!
Glühender Glanz
entgleisset dir weihlich im Wag!
Heia jahei! Heia jaheia!
Wache, Freund,
wache froh!
Wonnige Spiele
spenden wir dir:
flimmert der Fluss,
flammet die Flut,
umfliessen wir tauchend,
tanzend und singend,
im seligen Bade dein Bett!
Rheingold! Rheingold!
Heia jaheia! Heia jaheia!
Wallala la la la heia jahei!

ALBERICH
(dessen Augen, mächtig vom Glanze angezogen, starr an dem Golde haften).

Was ist's, ihr Glatten,
das dort so glänzt und gleisst?

DIE DREI RHEINTÖCHTER

Wo bist du Rauher denn heim,
dass vom Rheingold nicht du gehört?

WELLGUNDE

Nicht weiss der Alp
von des Goldes Auge,
das wechselnd wacht und schläft?

WOGLINDE

Von der Wassertiefe
wonnigem Stern,
der hehr die Wogen durchhellt?

DIE DREI RHEINTÖCHTER

Sieh, wie selig
im Glanze wir gleiten!
Willst du Banger
in ihm dich baden,
so schwimm' und schwelge mit uns!
Wallala la la leia lalei!
Wallala la la leia jahei!
(Sie lachen.)

ALBERICH

Eu'rem Taucherspiele
nur taugte das Gold?
Mir gält' es dann wenig!

WOGLINDE

Des Goldes Schmuck
schmähte er nicht,
wüsste er all seine Wunder!

WELLGUNDE

Der Welt Erbe
gewänne zu eigen,
wer aus dem Rheingold
schüfe den Ring,
der masslose Macht ihm verlieh'.

FLOSSHILDE

Der Vater sagt' es,
und uns befahl er,
klug zu hüten
den klaren Hort,
dass kein Falscher der Flut ihn entführe:
drum schweigt, ihr schwatzendes Heer!

WELLGUNDE

Du klügste Schwester,
verklag'st du uns wohl?
Weisst du denn nicht,
wem nur allein
das Gold zu schmieden vergönnt?

WOGLINDE

Nur wer der Minne
Macht entsagt,
nur wer der Minne
Lust verjagt,
nur'der erzielt sich den Zauber,
zum Reif zu zwingen das Gold.

WELLGUNDE

Wohl sicher sind wir
und sorgenfrei:
denn was nur lebt will lieben;
meiden will keiner die Minne.

WOGLINDE

Am wenigsten er,
der lüsterne Alp:
vor Liebesgier
möcht' er vergeh'n!

FLOSSHILDE

Nicht fürcht' ich den,
wie ich ihn erfand:
seiner Minne Brunst
brannte fast mich.

WELLGUNDE

Ein Schwefelbrand
in der Wogen Schwall:
vor Zorn der Liebe
zischt er laut!

DIE DREI RHEINTÖCHTER

Wallala! Wallaleia la la!
Lieblicher Albe!
lachst du nicht auch?

Rhinegold!
Luminous joy,
your laugh is so bright and rare!
Noble the gleam
that radiantly pierces the waves!
Heiajahei!
Heiajaheia!
Waken, friend!
Wake in joy!
Rapturous games
we'll gambol with you:
look at the flash
lighting the flood.
We float around diving,
dancing and singing,
and bathe in your glorious bed!
Rhinegold
Rhinegold!
Heiajaha!
Walalaleia jahei!

ALBERICH
*(whose eyes, fascinated by the light,
are fixed on the gold)*
What is it, you sleek ones,
so gleams and glows up there?

ALL THREE GIRLS
Have you not heard, you poor lout,
of the Rhinegold? Where were you born?

VELLGUNDA
The imp knows not
of the gold's bright eyes, then,
which wake and sleep, by turns?

VOGLINDA
Of the wondrous star
that gleams in the deep,
and nobly brightens the surge?

ALL THREE GIRLS
See how sweetly
we glide in its glances!
If you, faint-heart,
would bathe in glory,
then swim and revel with us.
(They laugh.)

ALBERICH
If the gold is worthless
except when you play,
I surely don't want it!

VOGLINDA
You would not scorn
gold of this kind
if you knew of its wonders.

VELLGUNDA
And world-rule is
the prize of the one
who out of the Rhinegold
fashions a ring
imparting a measureless might.

FLOSSHILDA
Our father said it,
and strictly bade us
guard the treasure
with cunning care,
that no swindler might greedily filch it.
So peace, you gossiping crew!

VELLGUNDA
O, clever sister,
you're blaming us both!
Do you not know
who is allowed
to use the gold as he will?

VOGLINDA
He who forswears
the power of love,
he who forswears
the joys of love:
that man alone finds the magic
to forge the gold to a ring.

VELLGUNDA
Why then, we are safe,
and need not fear,
for love rules all that's living:
nothing that lives flees affection.

VOGLINDA
And least of all he,
the lecherous imp,
who's nearly dead
panting for love.

FLOSSHILDA
I fear not him,
and I'm one to know
I was nearly scorched,
he was so hot.

VELLGUNDA
A brimstone brand
in the surging wave!
A lovesick passion
hissing aloud!

ALL THREE GIRLS
Walala! Walalcialala!
Loveliest elf-man!
Can't you laugh too?

In des Goldes Scheine
wie leuchtest du schön!
O komm', Lieblicher, lache mit uns!
Heia jaheia! Heia jaheia!
Wallala la la la leia jahei!
(Sie schwimmen lachend im Glanze auf und ab.)

ALBERICH
(die Augen starr auf das Gold gerichtet, hat dem Geplauder der Schwestern wohl gelauscht).

Der Welt Erbe
gewänn' ich zu eigen durch dich!
Erzwäng' ich nicht Liebe,
doch listig erzwäng' ich mir Lust?
(Furchtbar laut.)
Spottet nur zu! —
der Nibelung naht eurem Spiel!
(Wütend springt er nach dem mittleren Riff hinüber und klettert in grausiger Hast nach dessen Spitze hinauf. Die Mädchen fahren kreischend auseinander und tauchen nach verschiedenen Seiten hin auf.)

DIE DREI RHEINTÖCHTER
Heia! Heia! Heia jahei!
Rettet euch!
es raset der Alp;
in den Wassern sprüht's,
wohin er springt:
die Minne macht ihn verrückt!
Ha ha ha ha ha ha ha!
(Sie lachen im tollsten Übermut.)

ALBERICH
Bangt euch noch nicht?
So buhlt nun im Finstern,
feuchtes Gezücht!
(Er streckt die Hand nach dem Golde aus.)
Das Licht lösch' ich euch aus,
entreisse dem Riff das Gold,
schmiede den rächenden Ring;
denn hör' es die Flut:
so verfluch' ich die Liebe!
(Er reißt mit furchtbarer Gewalt das Gold aus dem Riffe und stürzt damit hastig in die Tiefe, wo er schnell verschwindet. Dichte Nacht bricht plötzlich überall herein. Die Mädchen tauchen jach dem Räuber in die Tiefe nach.)

FLOSSHILDE
Haltet den Räuber!

WELLGUNDE
Rettet das Gold!

DIE DREI RHEINTÖCHTER
Hülfe! Hülfe!
Weh'! Weh'!
(Die Flut fällt mit ihnen nach der Tiefe hinab, aus dem untersten Grunde hört man Alberichs gellendes Hohngelächter. In dichtester Finsternis verschwinden die Riffe; die ganze Bühne ist von der Höhe bis zur Tiefe von schwarzem Wassergewoge erfüllt, das eine Zeitlang immer noch abwärts zu sinken scheint.)

2. SZENE

Allmählich sind die Wogen in Gewölke übergegangen, welches, als eine immer heller dämmernde Beleuchtung dahinter tritt, zu feinerem Nebel sich abklärt. Als der Nebel in zarten Wölkchen gänzlich sich in der Höhe verliert, wird im Tagesgrauen eine

freie Gegend auf Bergeshöhen

sichtbar. — Der hervorbrechende Tag beleuchtet mit wachsendem Glanze eine Burg mit blinkenden Zinnen, die auf einem Felsgipfel im Hintergrunde steht: zwischen diesem burggekrönten Felsgipfel und dem Vordergrunde der Szene ist ein tiefes Tal, durch welches der Rhein fließt, anzunehmen. — Zur Seite auf blumigem Grunde liegt Wotan, neben ihm Fricka, beide schlafend. Die Burg ist ganz sichtbar geworden.

FRICKA
(erwacht; ihr Blick fällt auf die Burg; sie staunt und erschrickt.)

Wotan, Gemahl! erwache!

WOTAN
(im Traume leise)

Der Wonne seligen Saal
bewachen mir Tür' und Tor:
Mannes Ehre,
ewige Macht,
ragen zu endlosem Ruhm!

FRICKA
(rüttelt ihn)

Auf, aus der Träume
wonnigem Trug!
Erwache, Mann, und erwäge!

WOTAN
(erwacht und erhebt sich ein wenig, sein Auge wird sogleich vom Anblick der Burg gefesselt).

Vollendet das ewige Werk!
Auf Berges Gipfel
die Götterburg
prächtig prahlt
der prangende Bau!
Wie im Traum ich ihn trug,
wie mein Wille ihn wies,
stark und schön
steht er zur Schau;
hehrer, herrlicher Bau!

FRICKA

Nur Wonne schafft dir,
was mich erschreckt?
Dich freut die Burg,
mir bangt es um Freia!
Achtloser, lass dich erinnern
des ausbedungenen Lohns!

In the golden shimmer
how radiant you seem!
O come, lovely one,
join in our laugh!
(They laugh and sing, swimming up and down in the glow. Alberich's eyes are riveted on the gold.)

ALBERICH

So earth's kingdom
is mine to possess just through you?
If love be denied me,
yet pleasure is mine, if I'm smart!
(Very loud)
Mock as you will,
the Nibelung's near to your toy!
(Raging, he springs to the central rock and climbs it. The girls separate screaming and dart up in different directions.)

ALL THREE GIRLS

Heia! Heia! heiahahei!
Save yourselves!
The imp is quite mad!
How the water spurts
where he has sprung!
His love has made him insane!
(They laugh wildly.)

ALBERICH

Now do you fear?
Make love in the darkness,
fishified race!
(He reaches a greedy hand toward the gold.)
Your light now shall be quenched:
I'll plunder the guarded gold,
forging the ring of revenge.
So hear this, you waves:
I renounce love, and curse it!

(With terrible strength he tears the gold from the rock and, hastily descending, disappears below. Sudden darkness falls. The nymphs dive down after the robber.)

THE THREE GIRLS
(screaming)

Capture the robber!
Rescue the gold!
Help us! Help us!
Woe! Woe!
(The flood falls with them into the deep. Far below is heard Alberich's mocking laughter. Black waves seem to cover all.)

SCENE 2

Gradually the waves give place to clouds which clear off in fine mist, revealing

An Open Space on a Mountaintop

The dawning day lights up with growing luster a castle with glittering pinnacles, which stands on a cliff in the background: between this and the foreground is a deep valley through which the Rhine flows. At one side Wotan, king of the gods, and Fricka his wife are lying asleep in a flowery mead.

FRICKA
(wakes, and her eyes light on the castle. She gives a start.)

Wotan, my lord! Awaken!

WOTAN
(still dreaming)

My hall of blessed delight
is guarded at door and gate.
Manhood's honor,
infinite might,
towers to endless renown!

FRICKA
(shaking him)

Up from your dreams
of rosy deceit!
Awaken, lord, and consider!

(Wotan wakes and raises himself a little. His eyes are immediately riveted on the castle.)

WOTAN

The glorious work is achieved!
The gods' own castle
on mountain height!
Wondrous walls
of glittering pomp,
as I planned in my dream—
just the way I desired!
Strong and fair,
see how it looms:
lofty, lordly abode!

FRICKA

The joy you fashion
gives me alarm.
You love your hall:
my fears are for Freia!
Heedless one, try to remember
the price that has to be paid!

Die Burg ist fertig,
verfallen das Pfand:
vergassest du, was du vergabst?

WOTAN

Wohl dünkt mich's, was sie bedangen,
die dort die Burg mir gebaut;
durch Vertrag zähmt' ich
ihr trotzig Gezücht,
dass sie die hehre
Halle mir schüfen;
die steht nun — Dank den Starken —
um den Sold sorge dich nicht.

FRICKA

O lachend frevelnder Leichtsinn!
Liebelosester Frohmut!
Wüsst' ich um euren Vertrag,
dem Truge hätt' ich gewehrt;
doch mutig entferntet
ihr Männer die Frauen,
um taub und ruhig vor uns,
allein mit den Riesen zu tagen:
so ohne Scham
verschenktet ihr Frechen
Freia, mein holdes Geschwister,
froh des Schächergewerbs!

Was ist euch Harten
doch heilig und wert,
giert ihr Männer nach Macht!

WOTAN

Gleiche Gier
war Fricka wohl fremd,
als selbst um den Bau sie mich bat?

FRICKA

Um des Gatten Treue besorgt,
muss traurig ich wohl sinnen,
wie an mich er zu fesseln,
zieht's in die Ferne ihn fort:
herrliche Wohnung,
wonniger Hausrat,
sollten dich binden
zu säumender Rast.
Doch du bei dem Wohnbau sannst
auf Wehr und Wall allein:
Herrschaft und Macht
soll er dir mehren;
nur rastlosern Sturm zu erregen,
erstand dir die ragende Burg.

WOTAN
(lächelnd)

Wolltest du Frau
in der Feste mich fangen,
mir Gotte musst du schon gönnen,
dass, in der Burg
gebunden ich mir
von aussen gewinne die Welt.
Wandel und Wechsel
liebt wer lebt:
das Spiel drum kann ich nicht sparen!

FRICKA

Liebeloser,
leidigster Mann!
Um der Macht und Herrschaft
müssigen Tand
verspielst du in lästerndem Spott
Liebe und Weibes Wert?

WOTAN

Um dich zum Weib zu gewinnen,
mein eines Auge
setzt' ich werbend daran:
wie törig tadelst du jetzt!
Ehr' ich die Frauen
doch mehr, als dich freut!
Und Freia, die gute,
geb' ich nicht auf;
nie sann dies ernstlich mein Sinn.

FRICKA
(mit ängstlicher Spannung in die Szene blickend)

So schirme sie jetzt:
in schutzloser Angst
läuft sie nach Hülfe dort her!

FREIA
(tritt wie in hastiger Flucht auf)

Hilf mir, Schwester!
Schütze mich, Schwäher!
Vom Felsen drüben
drohte mir Fasolt,
mich Holde käm' er zu holen.

WOTAN

Lass ihn droh'n!
Sahst du nicht Loge?

FRICKA

Dass am liebsten du immer
dem Listigen traust!
Viel Schlimmes schuf er uns schon,
doch stets bestrickt er dich wieder.

WOTAN

Wo freier Mut frommt,
allein frag' ich nach keinem.
Doch des Feindes Neid

The castle's ready,
the payment is due.
Remember well what you pledged.

WOTAN

I mind well what they demanded,
I tamed them by
the bargain I made,
so that they built
the noblest of castles.
It stands now—thanks to the giants.
And the price? Think not of that.

FRICKA

Outrageous, laughable lightness!
Cheerful, hardhearted folly!
Had I but known of your deal,
I might have hindered the fraud,
the men though, in scorn
kept away from the women
—without confiding in us—
to talk all alone with the giants.
So without shame
you willingly
gave them Freia, my beautiful sister,
in this villainous deal!
What can you menfolk
see holy and good
once you're greedy for power!

WOTAN

Did not Fricka
harbor such greed
herself when she craved for the hall?

FRICKA

But I wished you faithful and true,
and sadly had to worry
how to keep you beside me
when you would stray far from home.
Halls great and lofty,
warm, household order—
these might entice you
to tarry at home.
But you in your fort
could think of only arms and war:
all to enhance
lordship and power.
And yet your majestical castle
but stands as a cradle of strife.

WOTAN
(smiling)

If you would keep me
confined in my fastness,
you yet must grant to my godhood
that, in the castle's confines
still I may conquer the world that's
    without.
Wandering and change
are loved by all.
I too must have some amusement!

FRICKA

Aggravating,
hardhearted man!
For the idle toys
of lordship and might
you'd gamble away in contempt
love and a woman's worth?

WOTAN

That time I wooed you to win you
I won by wager,
with an eye as the risk.
How foolish then to complain!
Women I honor,
still more than you like!
I'll never abandon
Freia the good.
I never held such a thought.

FRICKA
(looking away in anxious expectation)

Then save her right now:
her helpless distress
brings her here running.
            (Freia enters, as if in flight.)

FREIA

Help me, sister!
Save me, O, Wotan!
The giant scared me
near the great mountain,
and now he's coming to catch me.

WOTAN

Let him threat!
Have you seen Loge?

FRICKA

Tell me, why do you trust
in the treacherous god?
He's hurt us much through his tricks.
I see no end to his fooling.

WOTAN

Where honest strength serves
I ask no one for counsel.
But to turn the hate

zum Nutz sich fügen,
lehrt nur Schlauheit und List,
wie Loge verschlagen sie übt.
Der zum Vertrage mir riet,
versprach mir, Freia zu lösen:
auf ihn verlass' ich mich nun.

FRICKA

Und er lässt dich allein!
Dort schreiten rasch
die Riesen heran:
wo harrt dein schlauer Gehülf?

FREIA

Wo harren meine Brüder,
dass Hülfe sie brächten,
da mein Schwäher die Schwache verschenkt?
Zu Hülfe, Donner!
Hieher! hieher!
Rette Freia, mein Froh!

FRICKA

Die in bösem Bund dich verrieten,
sie alle bergen sich nun!

(Fasolt und Fafner in riesiger Gestalt, mit
starken Pfählen bewaffnet, treten auf)

FASOLT

Sanft schloss
Schlaf dein Aug';
wir beide bauten
Schlummers bar die Burg.
Mächt'ger Müh'
müde nie,
stauten starke
Stein' wir auf;
steiler Turm,
Tür' und Tor,
deckt und schliesst
im schlanken Schloss den Saal.
(Auf die Burg deutend.)
Dort steht's,
was wir stemmten,
schimmernd hell
bescheint's der Tag:
zieh nun ein,
uns zahl' den Lohn!

WOTAN

Nennt, Leute, den Lohn:
was dünkt euch zu bedingen?

FASOLT

Bedungen ist's,
was tauglich uns dünkt:
gemahnt es dich so matt?
Freia, die Holde,
Holda, die Freie —
vertragen ist's —
sie tragen wir heim.

WOTAN

Seid ihr bei Trost
mit eurem Vertrag?
Denkt auf andren Dank:
Freia ist mir nicht feil!

FASOLT

Was sagst du? ha!
Sinnst du Verrat?
Verrat am Vertrag?
Die dein Speer birgt,
sind sie dir Spiel,
des berat'nen Bundes Runen?

FAFNER

Getreu'ster Bruder,
merkst du Tropf nun Betrug?

FASOLT

Lichtsohn du,
leicht gefügter!
hör' und hüte dich:
Verträgen halte Treu'!
Was du bist,
bist du nur durch Verträge;
bedungen ist,
wohl bedacht deine Macht.
Bist weiser du
als witzig wir sind,
bandest uns Freie
zum Frieden du:
all deinem Wissen fluch' ich,
fliehe weit deinen Frieden,
weisst du nicht offen,
ehrlich und frei
Verträgen zu wahren die Treu'! —
Ein dummer Riese
rät dir das:
du Weiser, wiss' es von ihm!

WOTAN

Wie schlau für Ernst du achtest,
was wir zum Scherz nur beschlossen!

of foes to profit
needs both cunning and skill,—
a talent that Loge knows well.
He who arranged me this pact
has pledged the ransom for Freia.
I firmly trust in his skill.

FRICKA

And he leaves you alone.
The giants now
are striding this way,
so where's your cunning ally?

FREIA

Just what delays my brothers
from helping their sisters,
since my kinsman refuses to help?
O help me, Donner!
Hither, hither!
Rescue Freia, my Froh!

FRICKA

Through their wicked deal they betrayed
    you,
and now they hide from your sight.
*(Fasolt and Fafner, men of gigantic stature,
        armed with long staves, enter.)*

FASOLT

Soft sleep
sealed your eyes,
while we,
the sleepless workers, built your walls.
Mighty toil
tired us not.
Heavy stones
were heaped by us.
Towers rose,
doors and gates,
and at last
your fair and stately halls.
                (pointing to the castle)
There stands
what we built you,
shimmering bright
in light of day.
Enter in,
but pay our wage.

WOTAN

Men, tell us your price.
What payment was agreed on?

FASOLT

Agreed was
what we thought would be fair:
—Your memory is dull!—
Freia, the lovely,
Holda, the gracious.
The wage is this.
We're taking her home.

WOTAN
(quickly)

What is this?
Are you out of your mind?
Ask for something else.
Freia is not up for sale.

FASOLT

What *is* this? Ha!
Up to a trick?
Betraying your word?
What your spear holds,
is it in jest—
all those words of truth to bargains?

FAFNER

Most trusting brother,
any fool knows he's false.

FASOLT

Son of light,
light of honor,
hear, and heed yourself.
In bargains keep your word!
What you are,
are you only through treaties,
and all your might
well defined and precise.
More wise are you
than we are clever,
since you have bound us
to keep the peace.
Yet I must curse your wisdom.
Peace shall flee far from Wotan,
when you don't frankly,
fairly uphold
the terms of your contracts in truth!
A stupid giant
tells you this;
you wise one, take it from him!

WOTAN

How sly you are to take for truth
what was told you in jesting!

Die liebliche Göttin,
licht und leicht,
was taugt euch Tölpeln ihr Reiz?

FASOLT

Höhnst du uns?
Ha, wie unrecht! —
Die ihr durch Schönheit herrscht,
schimmernd hehres Geschlecht,
wie töricht strebt ihr
nach Türmen von Stein,
setzt um Burg und Saal
Weibes Wonne zum Pfand!
Wir Plumpen plagen uns
schwitzend mit schwieliger Hand,
ein Weib zu gewinnen,
das wonnig und mild
bei uns Armen wohne: —
und verkehrt nennst du den Kauf?

FAFNER

Schweig' dein faules Schwatzen.
Gewinn werben wir nicht:
Freias Haft
hilft wenig,
doch viel gilt's,
den Göttern sie zu entreissen.
Goldne Äpfel
wachsen in ihrem Garten,
sie allein
weiss die Äpfel zu pflegen;
der Frucht Genuss
frommt ihren Sippen
zu ewig nie
alternder Jugend;
siech und bleich
doch sinkt ihre Blüte,
alt und schwach
schwinden sie hin,
müssen Freia sie missen.
Ihrer Mitte drum sei sie entführt!

WOTAN
(für sich)

Loge säumt zu lang!

FASOLT

Schlicht gib nun Bescheid!

WOTAN

Sinnt auf andern Sold!

FASOLT

Kein andrer: Freia allein!

FAFNER

Du da, folge uns!

(Sie dringen auf Freia zu.)

FREIA

Helft! helft vor den Harten!

FROH
(Freia in seine Arme fassend)

Zu mir, Freia! —
Meide sie, Frecher!
Froh schützt die Schöne.

DONNER
(sich vor die beiden Riesen stellend)

Fasolt und Fafner,
fühltet ihr schon
meines Hammers harten Schlag?

FAFNER

Was soll das Droh'n?

FASOLT

Was dringst du her?
Kampf kiesten wir nicht,
verlangen nur unsern Lohn.

DONNER
(Er schwingt den Hammer.)

Schon oft zahlt' ich
Riesen den Zoll.
Kommt her, des Lohnes Last
wäg' ich mit gutem Gewicht!

WOTAN
*(seinen Speer zwischen den
Streitenden ausstreckend)*

Halt, du Wilder!
Nichts durch Gewalt!
Verträge schützt
meines Speeres Schaft:
spar' deines Hammers Heft!

FREIA

Wehe! Wehe!
Wotan verlässt mich!

FRICKA

Begreif ich dich noch,
grausamer Mann?

WOTAN
(wendet sich ab und sieht Loge kommen)

Endlich Loge!
Eiltest du so,

The goddess is lovely,
light and fair—
what use have dolts for her charms?

FASOLT

Must you flout?
Ha, how unjust,
you, who through beauty rule,
shimmering, radiant race!
Like fools you strive
for your towers of stone,
bartering for the work
glorious woman in pledge!
We doltheads drudge away,
sweating with callous-hard hands
to earn us a woman,
who'll grace with her charm the
homes of poor devils—
and you say all was a jest!

FAFNER

Hush your stupid chatter,
no prize comes from this deal.
Freia's charms help little.
It's much, though,
to seize her from the immortals.
Golden apples
grow and bloom in her garden.
She alone
knows the apples and tends them.
This goodly fruit
grants to her clansfolk
an endless youth
time cannot wither.
Sick and pale,
their beauty will vanish.
Soon they'll pass,
old and worn out
if their Freia is taken.
So I say we should carry her off!

WOTAN
(to himself)

Loge waits too long!

FASOLT

So, what shall it be?

WOTAN

Ask another wage.

FASOLT

No other: Freia alone!

FAFNER

You there, follow us!

*(Fafner and Fasolt press toward Freia. Froh
and Donner rush in.)*

FREIA

Help! Help from the hard-hearts!

FROH
(clasping Freia in his arms)

To me, Freia!
(to Fafner)
Off with you, villain!
Froh guards the fair one!

DONNER
(placing himself between the two giants)

Fasolt and Fafner,
What do you know
of my hammer's mighty blows?

FAFNER

What threat is this?

FASOLT

Why break in here?
Strife's not of our choice,
we only want what we've earned.

DONNER
(swinging his hammer)

I've given many
giants their pay.
Come here! A weighty wage
dealt in full measure is due.

WOTAN
*(interposing his spear
between the adversaries)*

Halt, you wild man!
Nothing through force!
All deals are kept
through my sacred spear.
Spare then your hammer's blow!

FREIA

Sorrow! Sorrow!
Wotan forsakes me!

FRICKA

Is this your intent,
terrible man?

WOTAN
(turning, he sees Loge coming)

Loge, finally!
Now you make haste,

den du geschlossen,
den schlimmen Handel zu schlichten?

LOGE
(ist im Hintergrunde aus dem Tale heraufgestiegen)

Wie? welchen Handel
hätt ich geschlossen?
Wohl was mit den Riesen
dort im Rate du dangst?
Zu Tiefen und Höhen
treibt mich mein Hang:
Haus und Herd
behagt mir nicht;
Donner und Froh,
die denken an Dach und Fach;
wollen sie frei'n,
ein Haus muss sie erfreu'n.
Ein stolzer Saal,
ein starkes Schloss,
danach stand Wotans Wunsch. —
Haus und Hof,
Saal und Schloss,
die selige Burg,
sie steht nun fest gebaut.
Das Prachtgemäuer
prüft' ich selbst,
ob alles fest,
forscht' ich genau:
Fasolt und Fafner
fand ich bewährt:
kein Stein wankt im Gestemm'.
Nicht müssig war ich,
wie mancher hier;
der lügt, wer lässig mich schilt!

WOTAN

Arglistig
weichst du mir aus:
mich zu betrügen
hüte in Treuen dich wohl!
Von allen Göttern
dein einz'ger Freund,
nahm ich dich auf
in den übel trauenden Tross. —
Nun red' und rate klug!
Da einst die Bauer der Burg
zum Dank Freia bedangen,
du weisst, nicht anders
willigt' ich ein,
als weil auf Pflicht du gelobtest,
zu lösen das hehre Pfand.

LOGE

Mit höchster Sorge
drauf zu sinnen,
wie es zu lösen,
das — hab' ich gelobt.
Doch, dass ich fände,
was nie sich fügt,
was nie gelingt, —
wie liess sich das wohl geloben?

FRICKA
(zu Wotan)

Sieh, welch trugvollem
Schelm du getraut!

FROH

Loge heisst du,
doch nenn' ich dich Lüge!

DONNER

Verfluchte Lohe,
dich lösch' ich aus!

LOGE

Ihre Schmach zu decken
schmähen mich Dumme.

(Donner holt auf Loge aus.)

WOTAN
(tritt dazwischen)

In Frieden lasst mir den Freund!
Nicht kennt ihr Loge's Kunst:
reicher wiegt
seines Rates Wert,
zahlt er zögernd ihn aus.

FAFNER

Nichts gezögert!
rasch gezahlt!

FASOLT

Lang währt's mit dem Lohn!

WOTAN
(wendet sich hart zu Loge, drängend)

Jetzt hör', Störrischer!
halte Stich!
Wo schweiftest du hin und her?

LOGE

Immer ist Undank
Loges Lohn!
Für dich nur besorgt,
sah ich mich um,
durchstöbert' im Sturm
alle Winkel der Welt,

thinking to straighten
the sorry business you handled?

LOGE
(ascending from the valley)

What? just what business
was it I handled!
Was it when you bargained
with the giants that time?
I'm driven by whim
to height and to depth.
House and hearth
attract me not.
Donner and Froh
have hankered for roof and rooms.
If they would woo,
a house first
they must own.
A lordly hall, a castle brave,
these have made Wotan's wish.
Roof and court,
tower and hall,
that blessed abode—
it stands now firm and sound.
I checked the lordly
walls myself
and all was sound,
perfectly made.
Fafner and Fasolt
kept to their word:
no stone's loose in the joints.
Nor was I idle,
like many here.
He lies, who says that I was!

WOTAN

Slyly you'd soften me up.
Try not to trick me,
stick to the facts as they are!
Of all the gods,
it was I alone
brought you as friend
to the crew that trusted you not.
Speak and show your skill!
The time the builders required
and asked Freia in payment,
you knew the reason
why I agreed:
because you solemnly promised
to ransom the glorious pledge.

LOGE

I said I'd do
some careful thinking
how to redeem it.
Yes, that I recall.
But, to discover
what never was
nor yet can be,
how could I make such a promise?

FRICKA
(to Wotan)

See what kind of a
rascal you trust!

FROH

Though you're Loge,
a better name's liar!

DONNER

Accursed fire,
I'll put you out!

LOGE

Just to mask your errors,
you scold me, blockheads!
(Donner and Froh threaten him.)

WOTAN
(warning them off)

Take care, don't bother my friend!
You know not Loge's art.
Rich advice
comes from his lips,
when we wait for his words.

FAFNER

No more waiting:
quick, our wage!

FASOLT

We've waited too long!

WOTAN
(to Loge)

Now hark, stubborn one!
Keep your word!
Why wander round here and there?

LOGE

I always meet
ingratitude!
Concerned for your sake,
hoping to help,
I scouted around
to the ends of the earth.

Ersatz für Freia zu suchen,
wie er den Riesen wohl recht.
Umsonst sucht' ich
und sehe nun wohl:
in der Welten Ring
nichts ist so reich,
als Ersatz zu muten dem Mann
für Weibes Wonne und Wert!

(Alle geraten in Erstaunen und verschiedenartige Betroffenheit.)

So weit Leben und Weben,
in Wasser, Erd' und Luft,
viel frug ich,
forschte bei allen,
wo Kraft nur sich rührt,
und Keime sich regen:
was wohl dem Manne
mächt'ger dünk'
als Weibes Wonne und Wert?
Doch so weit Leben und Weben,
verlacht nur ward
meine fragende List:
im Wasser, Erd' und Luft
lassen will nichts
von Lieb' und Weib.
Nur einen sah' ich
der sagte der Liebe ab:
um rotes Gold
entriet er des Weibes Gunst.
Des Rheines klare Kinder
klagten mir ihre Not:
der Nibelung
Nacht-Alberich,
buhlte vergebens
um der Badenden Gunst;
das Rheingold da
raubte sich rächend der Dieb:
das dünkt ihm nun
das teuerste Gut,
hehrer als Weibes Huld.
Um den gleissenden Tand,
der Tiefe entwandt,
erklang mir der Töchter Klage:
an dich, Wotan,
wenden sie sich,
dass zu Recht du zögest den Räuber,
das Gold dem Wasser
wieder gebest,
und ewig es bliebe ihr Eigen.

(Hingebende Bewegung aller.)

Dir's zu melden,
gelobt ich den Mädchen:
nun löste Loge sein Wort.

WOTAN

Törig bist du,
wenn nicht gar tückisch!
Mich selbst siehst du in Not:
wie hülf' ich andern zum Heil?

FASOLT
(der aufmerksam zugehört, zu Fafner)

Nicht gönn' ich das Gold dem Alben;
viel Not schuf uns der Niblung,
doch schlau entschlüpfte
unserm Zwange immer der Zwerg.

FAFNER

Neue Neidtat
sinnt uns der Niblung,
gibt das Gold ihm Macht. —
Du da, Loge!
Sag' ohne Lug:
was Grosses gilt denn das Gold,
dass dem Niblung es genügt?

LOGE

Ein Tand ist's
in des Wassers Tiefe,
lachenden Kindern zur Lust;
doch ward es zum runden
Reife geschmiedet,
hilft es zur höchsten Macht,
gewinnt dem Manne die Welt.

WOTAN
(sinnend)

Von des Rheines Gold
hört' ich raunen:
Beute-Runen
berge sein roter Glanz;
Macht und Schätze
schüf' ohne Mass ein Reif.

FRICKA
(leise zu Loge)

Taugte wohl
des goldnen Tandes
gleissend Geschmeid
auch Frauen zu schönem Schmuck?

LOGE

Des Gatten Treu'
ertrotzte die Frau,
trüge sie hold
den hellen Schmuck,
den schimmernd Zwerge schmieden,
rührig im Zwange des Reifs.

FRICKA

Gewänne mein Gatte
sich wohl das Gold?

I sought a ransom for Freia
such as the giants might like.
I sought vainly,
and plainly now see
in the whole wide world
nothing's so hard
to replace in heart of a man
as woman's sweetness and worth!
(All exhibit surprise and various emotions.)
I asked everything living
in water and earth and air,
this question,
ever inquiring,
where nature puts forth,
and seedlings are stirring:
what does a man
hold mightier still
than woman's beauty and worth?
But in all places I went to,
my cunning question
was greeted with laughs.
In water, earth and air
female and love
are all their care.
Just one I met with
had really cast love aside,
He gave it up
for sake of some ruddy gold.
The Rhine's bright-gleaming children
clamored woe in my ears.
The Nibelung,
Night-Alberich,
courted the girls,
hoping for grace, but in vain.
The Rhinegold he
robbed them in thievish revenge.
He thinks it now
the worthiest good,
greater than woman's grace.
For their glittering toy,
thus torn from the deep,
the daughters make such lamenting,
To you, Wotan,
turning in prayers
to let justice fall on the robber,
and so return
their treasure to them,
to rest in their waters forever.
This I promised
to speak of to Wotan,
and this has Loge performed.

WOTAN

You are either
a fool or deceiver!

I'm in trouble myself,
how can I help someone else?

FASOLT
(to Fafner)

I grudge giving gold to Alberich.
He's done much damage already.
His cunning, though,
has kept him safely out of our clutch.

FAFNER

New despite
will come from the dwarf—
now gold has brought him power.
You there, Loge,
say without lies
what power is lodged in this gold
that it satisfies the dwarf.

LOGE

A toy merely,
within deep waters,
serving the children for sport.
Yet when it is fashioned
into
a circlet
it will give highest power
and grant its owner the earth.

WOTAN
(thoughtfully)

I have heard
some rumors about it:
runes of riches
hide in its ruddy gleam.
Boundless power
and wealth will the ring bestow.

FRICKA
(softly to Loge)

Would the golden trinket
make some glittering gear
for women to wear in show?

LOGE

A wife would keep
her husband quite true
could she but win
the trick of that gold,
so brightly forged by Nibelungs,
servants and slaves to the ring.

FRICKA
(coaxingly to Wotan)

I wish that my lord
could come by the gold!

WOTAN
(wie in einem Zustande wachsender Bezauberung)

Des Reifes zu walten,
rätlich will es mich dünken.
Doch wie, Loge,
lernt' ich die Kunst?
wie schüf ich mir das Geschmeid?

LOGE

Ein Runenzauber
zwingt das Gold zum Reif;
keiner kennt ihn;
doch einer übt ihn leicht,
der sel'ger Lieb' entsagt.
(Wotan wendet sich unmutig ab.)
Das sparst du wohl;
zu spät auch kämst du:
Alberich zauderte nicht.
Zaglos gewann er
des Zaubers Macht:
geraten ist ihm der Ring!

DONNER
(zu Wotan)

Zwang uns allen
schüfe der Zwerg,
würd' ihm der Reif nicht entrissen.

WOTAN

Den Ring muss ich haben!

FROH

Leicht erringt
ohne Liebesfluch er sich jetzt.

LOGE

Spott-leicht,
ohne Kunst wie im Kinder-Spiel!

WOTAN
(grell)

So rate, wie?

LOGE

Durch Raub!
Was ein Dieb stahl,
das stiehlst du dem Dieb:
ward leichter ein Eigen erlangt?
Doch mit arger Wehr
wahrt sich Alberich;
klug und fein
musst du verfahren,
ziehst den Räuber du zu Recht,
um des Rheines Töchtern,
den roten Tand,
(Mit Wärme.)
das Gold wieder zu geben:
denn darum flehen sie dich.

WOTAN

Des Rheines Töchtern?
Was taugt mir der Rat?

FRICKA

Von dem Wassergezücht
mag ich nichts wissen:
schon manchen Mann —
mir zum Leid! —
verlockten sie buhlend im Bad.
(Wotan steht stumm mit sich kämpfend; die übrigen Götter heften in schweigender Spannung die Blicke auf ihn. Währenddem hat Fafner beiseite mit Fasolt beraten.)

FAFNER
(zu Fasolt)

Glaub' mir, mehr als Freia
frommt das gleissende Gold:
auch ew'ge Jugend erjagt,
wer durch Goldes Zauber sie zwingt.
(Fasolts Gebärde deutet an, daß er sich wider Willen überredet fühlt. Fafner tritt mit Fasolt wieder an Wotan heran.)
Hör', Wotan,
der Harrenden Wort!
Freia bleib' euch in Frieden;
leichter'n Lohn
fand ich zur Lösung:
uns rauhen Riesen genügt
des Niblungen rotes Gold.

WOTAN

Seid ihr bei Sinn?
Was nicht ich besitze,
soll ich euch Schamlosen schenken?

FAFNER

Schwer baute
dort sich die Burg:
leicht wird's dir
mit list'ger Gewalt
(was im Neidspiel nie uns gelang):
den Niblungen fest zu fah'n.

WOTAN

Für euch müht' ich
mich um den Alben?
Für euch fing' ich den Feind?
Unverschämt
und übergehrlich
macht euch Dumme mein Dank!

(Wotan appears more and more bewitched with his thought.)

WOTAN

Control of that circlet
might be wise, to my thinking.
Yet how, Loge,
could it be done—
how shape the thing for my ends?

LOGE

Some rune of magic
makes the gold a ring.
No one knows it.
It's easy though to learn
by him who forswears love.
(Wotan turns away discouraged.)
That suits you not—
too late for you, too.
Alberich wasted no time.
Fearless, he won
the magic's might:
success was his with the ring.

DONNER
(to Wotan)

We should wrest
the ring from the dwarf,
else we will all be his servants.

WOTAN

That ring I must capture!

FROH

Now it's easy
to win without cursing love.

LOGE
(harshly)

Quite easy,
it's child's play—no art required!

WOTAN

Advise us, how?

LOGE

By theft!
What a thief stole,
that steal from the thief.
How easy to come by one's own!
Yet the Nibelung
is skilled in wicked aims.
What you do
has to be clever,
if you'd overcome the thief,
so the Rhine-god's daughters
may have their ruddy gold
once more to play with—
for which they're crying to you.

WOTAN

The Rhine-god's daughters?
What nonsense is this?

FRICKA

Oh, that watery brood
makes me offended:
for many men—
I'm sad to say—
have perished, allured to their bath.

FAFNER
(to Fasolt)

Trust me, glittering gold
like that is better than she.
Besides, the magical gold
brings eternal youth with its power.
Hear, Wotan, our very last words!
Let your Freia remain here.
Smaller payment
now will suit us.
We clumsy giants want
only gold of the Nibelung hoard.

WOTAN

Have you gone mad?
Just how can I grant you
what is not mine yet, you rascals?

FAFNER

Hard work went
into that fort.
Quite simply,
with cunning control
(which our might could never achieve)
you'll fetter the Nibelung fast.

WOTAN

For *you* should I
bother with Alberich?
For *you* fetter the foe?
Unashamed,
with all too much greed,
my kindness turned you to clowns!

FASOLT
*(ergreift plötzlich Freia und führt sie mit
Fafner zur Seite)*

Hieher, Maid!
In unsre Macht!
Als Pfand folgst du uns jetzt,
bis wir Lösung empfah'n!

FREIA
(wehklagend)

Wehe! Wehe! Weh'!
(Alle Götter sind in höchster Bestürzung.)

FAFNER

Fort von hier
sei sie entführt!
Bis Abend — achtet's wohl! —
pflegen wir sie als Pfand:
wir kehren wieder;
doch kommen wir,
und bereit liegt nicht als Lösung
das Rheingold licht und rot —

FASOLT

Zu End' ist die Frist dann,
Freia verfallen:
für immer folge sie uns!

FREIA
(schreiend)

Schwester! Brüder!
Rettet! Helft!
*(Sie wird von den hastig enteilenden Riesen
fortgetragen.)*

FROH

Auf, ihnen nach!

DONNER

Breche denn alles!
(Sie blicken Wotan fragend an.)

FREIA
(aus weiter Ferne)

Rettet! Helft!

LOGE
(den Riesen nachsehend)

Über Stock und Stein zu Tal
stapfen sie hin:
durch des Rheines Wasserfurt
waten die Riesen.
Fröhlich nicht
hängt Freia
den Rauhen über dem Rücken! —

Heia! hei!
Wie taumeln die Tölpel dahin!
Durch das Tal talpen sie schon.
Wohl an Riesenheim's Mark
erst halten sie Rast —
(Er wendet sich zu den Göttern.)
Was sinnt nun Wotan so wild?
Den sel'gen Göttern wie geht's?
*(Ein fahler Nebel erfüllt mit wachsender Dicht-
heit die Bühne; in ihm erhalten die Götter ein zu-
nehmend bleiches und ältliches Aussehen: alle stehen
bang und erwartungsvoll auf Wotan blickend,
der sinnend die Augen an den Boden heftet.)*
Trügt mich ein Nebel?
Neckt mich ein Traum?
Wie bang und bleich
verblüht ihr so bald!
Euch erlischt der Wangen Licht;
der Blick eures Auges verblitzt!
Frisch, mein Froh!
noch ist's ja früh!
Deiner Hand, Donner,
entsinkt ja der Hammer!
Was ist's mit Fricka?
freut sie sich wenig
ob Wotans grämlichem Grau,
das schier zum Greisen ihn schafft?

FRICKA

Wehe! Wehe!
Was ist gescheh'n?

DONNER

Mir sinkt die Hand!

FROH

Mir stockt das Herz!

LOGE

Jetzt fand ich's: hört, was euch fehlt!
Von Freias Frucht
genosset ihr heute noch nicht.
Die goldnen Äpfel
in ihrem Garten
sie machten euch tüchtig und jung,
asst ihr sie jeden Tag.
Des Gartens Pflegerin
ist nun verpfändet:
an den Ästen darbt
und dorrt das Obst:
bald fällt faul es herab. —
Mich kümmert's minder;
an mir ja kargte
Freia von je
knauserndd die köstliche Frucht:

FASOLT
*(suddenly seizes Freia and draws
her to one side with Fafner)*

This way, girl!
You're in our power!
Just come, you are our pledge
till the ransom arrives.

FREIA
(shrieking)

Help me! Save me! Woe!

FAFNER

We shall take her
far from here!
Till evening, mark me well—
know, she stands as a pledge.
We're coming back, though,
so wait for us,
and unless you give in ransom
the Rhinegold fair and red—

FASOLT
(interrupting)

The time will be ended,
Freia will leave you
as ours, and never come back.

FREIA
(crying out)

Sister! Brothers!
Save me! Help!
*(She is dragged away by the hastily retreating
giants.)*

FROH

After her, quick!

DONNER

Everything's ruined!
(They look inquiringly at Wotan.)

FREIA
(in the distance)

Save me! Help!

LOGE
(looking after the giants)

Over stick and stone they stride
down through the vale.
Through the shallows of the Rhine
see how they are wading.
Freia hangs,
sad, joyless,
upon the backs of the roughnecks!
Heia! Hi!
The blockheads are stumbling along!
There they stalk, right through the vale.
(He turns to the gods.)

What thought makes Wotan so wild?
Alas, what's ailing the gods?
*(A pale mist, that grows denser and denser,
fills the air. As they stand in it, the gods seem
to become wan and aged. Alarmed, they
watch Wotan, who is gazing thoughtfully at
the ground.)*

Is there a mist here?
You've grown so withered,
fearful and pale,
and the bloom has fled your cheeks.
The light of your eyes has gone out!
Quick, my Froh!
Day is still young!
From your hand, Donner,
the hammer is falling!
What's wrong with Fricka?
Can she be grieving
at Wotan's gloomy decline
that makes him suddenly old?

FRICKA

Woe's me! Woe's me!
What has gone wrong?

DONNER

My hand has sunk!

FROH

My heart has stopped!

LOGE

I have it! Learn what you're lacking!
You've had no taste
of Freia's fine apples today.
The golden apples
from out her garden
have kept you all hearty and young—
eating them every day.
The gardener's guardian
has now been kidnaped.
On the branches starves
and dries the fruit.
You'll soon see it decay.
My worry is less,
for Freia was always
stingy with me,
grudging the exquisite fruit.

denn halb so echt nur
bin ich wie, Selige, ihr!
Doch ihr setztet alles
auf das jüngende Obst:
das wussten die Riesen wohl;
auf euer Leben
legten sie's an:
nun sorgt, wie ihr das wahrt!
Ohne die Äpfel,
alt und grau,
greis und grämlich,
welkend zum Spott aller Welt,
erstirbt der Götter Stamm.

FRICKA
(bang)

Wotan, Gemahl!
unsel'ger Mann!
Sieh, wie dein Leichtsinn
lachend uns allen
Schimpf und Schmach erschuf!

WOTAN
(mit plötzlichem Entschluß auffahrend)

Auf, Loge!
hinab mit mir!
Nach Nibelheim fahren wir nieder:
gewinnen will ich das Gold.

LOGE

Die Rheintöchter
riefen dich an;
so dürfen Erhörung sie hoffen?

WOTAN

Schweige, Schwätzer!
Freia, die Gute,
Freia gilt es zu lösen!

LOGE

Wie du befiehlst,
führ' ich dich gern:
steil hinab
steigen wir denn durch den Rhein?

WOTAN

Nicht durch den Rhein!

LOGE

So schwingen wir uns
durch die Schwefelkluft:

dort schlüpfe mit mir hinein!
(Er geht voran und verschwindet seitwärts in einer Kluft, aus der sogleich ein schwefliger Dampf hervorquillt.)

WOTAN

Ihr andern harrt
bis Abend hier:
verlor'ner Jugend
erjag' ich erlösendes Gold!
(Er steigt Loge nach in die Kluft hinab: der aus ihr dringende Schwefeldampf verbreitet sich über die ganze Bühne und erfüllt diese schnell mit dickem Gewölk. Bereits sind die Zurückbleibenden unsichtbar.)

DONNER

Fahre wohl, Wotan!

FROH

Glück auf! Glück auf!

FRICKA

O kehre bald
zur bangenden Frau!

(Der Schwefeldampf verdüstert sich bis zu ganz schwarzem Gewölk, welches von unten nach oben steigt; dann verwandelt sich dieses in festes, finstres Steingeklüft, das sich immer aufwärts bewegt, so daß es den Anschein hat, als sänke die Szene immer tiefer in die Erde hinab. Wachsendes Geräusch wie von Schmiedenden wird überallher vernommen.)

3. SZENE

Von verschiedenen der Seiten her dämmert aus Ferne dunkelroter Schein auf: eine unabsehbar weit sich dahinziehende

unterirdische Kluft

wird erkennbar, die nach allen Seiten hin in enge Schachte auszumünden scheint.

Alberich zerrt den kreischenden Mime an den Ohren aus einer Seitenschlucht herbei.

ALBERICH

Hehe! hehe!
hieher! hieher!
Tückischer Zwerg!
Tapfer gezwickt
sollst du mir sein,
schaffst du nicht fertig,
wie ich's bestellt,
zur Stund' das feine Geschmeid'!

For all I have
is half of the lineage of gods.
Yet you trusted wholly
to the apples of youth.
The giants perceived this well.
They got together,
plotting your death.
So give thought to your defense.
Lacking the apples,
old and gray,
sad and sullen,
shriveled, a scorn to the world,
the race of gods must cease.

FRICKA
(in dread)

Wotan, my lord!
Unhappy man!
See how your light
and frivolous thoughts
have brought us shame and scorn!

WOTAN
(starting up with sudden resolution)

Up, Loge,
and off with me!
We now must descend to the Nibelungs!
I'm going to ravish the gold.

LOGE

The Rhine-daughters
called for your help,
so may they expect restitution?

FRICKA

Quiet, babbler!
Freia, the noble,
Freia now must be rescued.

LOGE

As you command,
so shall I lead.
Shall we go
down by the way of the Rhine?

WOTAN

Not through the Rhine!

LOGE

We'll swing ourselves
right through the brimstone.
Just slip that way with me now!
(He goes ahead and disappears at the side down a crevice, from which immediately a sulphurous vapor rises.)

WOTAN

You others, wait
till evening here.
Our youth that left us
returns when I ravish the gold.
(He clambers after Loge into the cleft. The sulphurous vapor increases.)

DONNER

Fare you well, Wotan!

FROH

Good luck! Good luck!

FRICKA

O come back soon
to her who's afraid.

(The sulfurous vapor thickens to a black cloud. This changes to solid dark rocky chasms, which also move upward. From various quarters ruddy gleams shine out in the distance: an increasing clamor of smithies is heard around. The clang of the anvils dies away. A subterranean cavern, stretching farther than the eye can reach, is now visible, on all sides opening on to narrow passages.)

Scene 3

Nibelhome

(Alberich enters, dragging the shrieking Mime from a cleft)

ALBERICH

He-he! He-he!
Come here! Come here!
Rascally dwarf!
Think of the nips
coming your way,
should you not hurry,
as I command,
to forge the delicate work!

MIME
(heulend)

Ohe! Ohe!
Au! Au!
Lass mich nur los!
Fertig ist's,
wie du befahlst,
mit Fleiss und Schweiss
ist es gefügt:
nimm nur die Nägel vom Ohr!

ALBERICH

Was zögerst du dann,
und zeigst es nicht?

MIME

Ich Armer zagte,
dass noch was fehle.

ALBERICH

Was wär' noch nicht fertig?

MIME
(verlegen)

Hier ... und da ...

ALBERICH

Was hier und da?
Her das Geschmeid'!

(Er will ihm wieder an das Ohr fahren; vor Schreck läßt Mime ein metallenes Gewirke, das er krampfhaft in den Händen hielt, sich entfallen. Alberich hebt es hastig auf und prüft es genau.)

Schau, du Schelm!
Alles geschmiedet
und fertig gefügt,
wie ich's befahl!
So wollte der Tropf
schlau mich betrügen,
für sich behalten
das hehre Geschmeid',
das meine List
ihn zu schmieden gelehrt?
Kenn' ich dich dummen Dieb?

(Er setzt das Gewirk als „Tarnhelm" auf den Kopf.)

Dem Haupt fügt sich der Helm:
ob sich der Zauber auch zeigt?

(Sehr leise.)

"Nacht und Nebel —
niemand gleich!"

(Seine Gestalt verschwindet; statt ihrer gewahrt man eine Nebelsäule.)

Siehst du mich, Bruder?

MIME
(blickt sich verwundert um)

Wo bist du? ich sehe dich nicht.

ALBERICH
(unsichtbar)

So fühle mich doch,
du fauler Schuft!
Nimm das für dein Diebsgelüst!

MIME
(schreit und windet sich unter empfangenen Geißelhieben, deren Fall man vernimmt, ohne die Geißel selbst zu sehen)

Ohe! Ohe!
Au! Au! Au!

ALBERICH

Haha haha haha!
Hab' Dank, du Dummer!
Dein Werk bewährt sich gut!
Hoho! Hoho!
Nibelungen all',
neigt euch nun Alberich!
Überall weilt er nun,
euch zu bewachen;
Ruh' und Rast
ist euch zerronnen;
ihm müsst ihr schaffen,
wo nicht ihr ihn schaut;
wo ihr nicht ihn gewahrt,
seid seiner gewärtig!
Untertan seid ihr ihm immer!
Hoho! Hoho!
hört ihn, er naht;
der Niblungen Herr!

(Die Nebelsäule verschwindet dem Hintergrunde zu: man hört in immer weiterer Ferne Alberichs Toben und Zanken; Geheul und Geschrei antwortet ihm, das sich endlich in immer weitere Ferne unhörbar verliert. Mime ist vor Schmerz zusammengesunken. Wotan und Loge lassen sich aus einer Schlucht von oben herab.)

LOGE

Nibelheim hier:
durch bleiche Nebel
was blitzen dort feurige Funken?

MIME

Au! Au! Au!

WOTAN

Hier stöhnt es laut:
was liegt im Gestein?

MIME
(howling)

Ohe! Ohe!
Oh! Oh!
Let me alone!
All's been done
just as you asked.
My toil and sweat
molded the work.
Take out your nails from my ear.

ALBERICH

Then why the delay
to show it me?

MIME

I feared that something
you wished was lacking.

ALBERICH

Why was it not ready?

MIME
(hesitating)

Here and there.

ALBERICH

How "here and there"?
Hand me the work.

(He threatens Mime's ear again. The latter, terrified, lets fall a piece of metalwork. Alberich picks it up and examines it.)

Look, you scamp!
All has been fitted
and carefully forged,
just as I wished.
A plague on the rogue!
Would he deceive me
to keep the beautiful
work for himself,
work that my cunning
had taught him?
Do I not know you, thief?

(He sets the metalwork on his head as a "Tarnhelm.")

The helm fits to the head,
but will its magic prove good?
(very softly)
Night and darkness,
hide from me now!

(His form disappears, replaced by a column of vapor.)

See me, O brother?

MIME
(looking around, astonished)

Where are you? I see you no more.

ALBERICH
(invisible)

Then feel me instead,
you wicked scamp!
(Mime writhes under blows from an invisible scourge.)
Take that for your thievish greed!

MIME

Ohe! Ohe!
Oh! Oh! Oh!

ALBERICH

Ha ha ha ha ha ha!
I thank you, numbskull,
your work is tried and true!
Ho ho! Ho ho!
Nibelung elves,
bow down to Alberich!
Now he is everywhere,
watching and spying.
Peace and rest
now have been banished.
Work for your master,
who watches unseen,
and when least you're aware
sees all of your actions.
You're his slaves,
now and forever.
Ho ho! Ho ho!
Hear him, he comes:
the Nibelung lord!

(The column of vapor disappears. Alberich's scoldings retreat in the distance. Mime has cowered down in pain. Wotan and Loge descend from above by a shaft.)

LOGE

Nibelhome's here.
The glare is seen
through the darkness in fiery vapors.

MIME

Oh! Oh! Oh!

WOTAN

Who groans so loud?
What lies on the stones?

LOGE
(neigt sich zu Mime)
Was Wunder wimmerst du hier?

MIME
Ohe! Ohe! Au! Au!

LOGE
Hei, Mime! Munt'rer Zwerg!
Was zwickt und zwackt dich denn so?

MIME
Lass mich in Frieden!

LOGE
Das will ich freilich,
und mehr noch, hör':
helfen will ich dir, Mime!
(Er stellt ihn mühsam aufrecht.)

MIME
Wer hälfe mir!
Gehorchen muss ich
dem leiblichen Bruder,
der mich in Bande gelegt.

LOGE
Dich, Mime, zu binden,
was gab ihm die Macht?

MIME
Mit arger List
schuf sich Alberich
aus Rheines Gold
einen gelben Reif:
seinem starken Zauber
zittern wir staunend;
mit ihm zwingt er uns alle,
der Niblungen nächt'ges Heer.
Sorglose Schmiede,
schufen wir sonst wohl
Schmuck unsern Weibern,
wonnig Geschmeid',
niedlichen Niblungentand:
wir lachten lustig der Müh'.
Nun zwingt uns der Schlimme,
in Klüfte zu schlüpfen,
fur ihn allein
uns immer zu müh'n.
Durch des Ringes Gold
errät seine Gier,
wo neuer Schimmer
in Schachten sich birgt:
da müssen wir spähen,
spüren und graben,
die Beute schmelzen,
und schmieden den Guss,
ohne Ruh' und Rast
dem Herrn zu häufen den Hort.

LOGE
Dich Trägen soeben
traf wohl sein Zorn?

MIME
Mich Ärmsten, ach!
mich zwang er zum Ärgsten:
ein Helmgeschmeid'
hiess er mich schweissen;
genau befahl er,
wie es zu fügen.
Wohl merkt' ich klug,
welch' mächt'ge Kraft
zu eigen dem Werk,
das aus Erz ich wob;
für mich drum hüten
wollt' ich den Helm;
durch seinen Zauber
Alberichs Zwang mich entzieh'n:
vielleicht — ja vielleicht
den Lästigen selbst überlisten,
in meine Gewalt ihn zu werfen,
den Ring ihm zu entreissen,
dass, wie ich Knecht jetzt dem Kühnen,
(Greil.)
mir Freien er selber dann fröhn'!

LOGE
Warum, du Kluger,
glückte dir's nicht?

MIME
Ach! der das Werk ich wirkte,
den Zauber, der ihn entzückt,
den Zauber erriet ich nicht recht!
Der das Werk mir riet,
und mir's entriss,
der lehrte mich nun
— doch leider zu spät, —
welche List läg' in dem Helm.
Meinem Blick entschwand er;
doch Schwielen dem Blinden
schlug unschaubar sein Arm.
(Heulend und schluchzend.)
Das schuf ich mir Dummen
schön zu Dank!

LOGE
(bending over Mime)
What marvel's whimpering here?

MIME
Ohe! Ohe! Oh! Oh!

LOGE
Hey, Mime! Merry dwarf!
What beats and teases you thus?

MIME
Leave me in quiet!

LOGE
That will I gladly,
and more yet, hear!
Help is coming now, Mime.
(He sets him carefully on his feet.)

MIME
But help from whom?
I have for master
the truest of brothers,
who's bound me fast through his might.

LOGE
But Mime, what gave him
the might of command?

MIME
With wicked craft
Alberich made
a magic ring
from gold from the river Rhine.
At its magic spell
we tremble, astonished.
He thus puts in his power
the Nibelung gnomes of might.
Once, in our carefree,
smithing days
we made gear
for our women,
winsomely forged,
delicate Nibelung toys.
We laughed with joy as we toiled.
This wretch now compels us
to slip into chasms.
We're always toiling
only for him.
Through the ring of gold,
he sees in his greed
where shining ore
has been hid in the pits.
And then we must seek it,
find it and dig it,
then smelt the booty,
and forge it to shapes.
With no peace nor pause
we heap the hoard for our lord.

LOGE
Your idleness may have
roused him to wrath.

MIME
I'm wretched, ah!
He treats me most cruelly,
I did as told,
forged him a helmet.
He told me in detail
how I should make it.
I shrewdly sensed
the mighty power
instinct in that work,
which I wove of ore.
I wished to keep
the helm for myself,
and with its magic
whisk away Alberich's power.
Perhaps—yes—perhaps
I even might outwit the bully,
subduing his might to my power,
and then with the ring ravished,
I, who had once been the bondsman,
as freeman thence should command!

LOGE
Then why, my plotter,
had you not luck?

MIME
Ah, though I forged the wonder,
the magic that gave him joy,
that magic I read not aright.
He who planned my work
then stole my work!
And now to my grief
I found out too late
of the charm hid in the helm.
While I looked he vanished!
But though I was blind,
the blows he gave me were seen!
(howling and sobbing)
And such is the thanks
this fool has won!

DAS RHEINGOLD

LOGE
(zu Wotan)

Gesteh', nicht leicht
gelingt der Fang.

WOTAN

Doch erliegt der Feind,
hilft deine List!

MIME
(betrachtet aufmerksamer die Götter)

Mit eurem Gefrage,
wer seid denn ihr Fremde?

LOGE

Freunde dir;
von ihrer Not
befrei'n wir der Niblungen Volk!

MIME
*(schrickt zusammen, da er Alberich sich
wieder nahen hört)*

Nehmt euch in acht!
Alberich naht.

WOTAN

Sein' harren wir hier.

*(Er setzt sich ruhig auf einen Stein; Loge lehnt
ihm zur Seite. Alberich, der den Tarnhelm vom
Haupte genommen und an den Gürtel gehängt
hat, treibt mit geschwungener Geißel aus der un-
teren, tiefer gelegenen Schlucht aufwärts eine Schar
Nibelungen vor sich her: diese sind mit goldenem
und silbernem Geschmeide beladen, das sie, unter
Alberichs steter Nötigung, all auf einen Haufen
speichern und so zu einem Horte häufen.)*

ALBERICH

Hieher! Dorthin!
Hehe! Hoho!
Träges Heer!
Dort zu Hauf
schichtet den Hort!
Du da, hinauf!
Willst du voran?
Schmähliches Volk!
Ab das Geschmeide!
Soll ich euch helfen?
Alles hieher!

(Er gewahrt plötzlich Wotan und Loge.)

He! wer ist dort?
Wer drang hier ein?
Mime, zu mir!
Schäbiger Schuft!
Schwatzest du gar
mit dem schweifenden Paar?

Fort, du Fauler!
Willst du gleich schmieden und schaffen?

*(Er treibt Mime mit Geißelhieben unter den
Haufen der Nibelungen hinein.)*

He! an die Arbeit!
Alle von hinnen!
Hurtig hinab!
Aus den neuen Schachten
schafft mir das Gold!
Euch grüsst die Geissel,
grabt ihr nicht rasch!
Dass keiner mir müssig,
bürge mir Mime,
sonst birgt er sich schwer
meiner Geissel Schwunge!
Dass ich überall weile,
wo keiner mich wähnt,
das weiss er, dünkt mich, genau!
Zögert ihr noch?
Zaudert wohl gar?

*(Er zieht seinen Ring vom Finger, küßt ihn
und streckt ihn drohend aus.)*

Zitt're und zage,
gezähmtes Heer!
Rasch gehorcht
des Ringes Herrn!

*(Unter Geheul und Gekreisch stieben die Nibe-
lungen, unter ihnen Mime, auseinander und schlüpfen in die Schächte hinab.)*

ALBERICH
*(betrachtet lange und mißtrauisch
Wotan und Loge).*

Was wollt ihr hier?

WOTAN

Von Nibelheims nächt'gem Land
vernahmen wir neue Mär':
mächt'ge Wunder
wirke hier Alberich;
daran uns zu weiden,
trieb uns Gäste die Gier.

ALBERICH

Nach Nibelheim
führt euch der Neid;
so kühne Gäste,
glaubt, kenn' ich gut!

LOGE

Kennst du mich gut,
kindischer Alp?
Nun sag', wer bin ich,
dass du so bellst?
Im kalten Loch,
da kauernd du lagst,
wer gab dir Licht
und wärmende Lohe,

LOGE
(to Wotan)

Admit, it's not
an easy job.

WOTAN

Yet the foes will fall,
thanks to your art.
(Mime observes the gods more attentively.)
But who are you, strangers,
that ask me these questions?

LOGE

Friends of yours.
We wish to free
the Nibelung folk from their woe.
(Hearing Alberich approach, Mime crouches down.)

MIME

Keep a sharp look,
Alberich comes.
(He runs hither and yon in terror.)

WOTAN
(seating himself on a stone)

We'll wait your lord here.

(Alberich, who has taken off the Tarnhelm and hung it in his girdle, drives with brandished scourge from the caves below a crowd of Nibelungs before him. They are laden with gold and silver jewelry, which, under Alberich's continued urging, they pile up to form a hoard.)

ALBERICH

Hither, thither!
He-he! Ho-ho!
Lazy gang!
There in heaps
pile up the hoard!
You there, get up!
Will you move on?
Scandalous folk!
Off with the treasure!
Need any help there?
All of it here!
(He suddenly perceives Wotan and Loge.)
Hey! Who is there?
Intruders here?
Mime, come here,
scabby old scamp!
Babbling like this
with a vagabond pair!

Off, you no-good!
Off to your forging and welding!
(He drives Mime with blows of his scourge into the gang of Nibelungs.)
Hey, get to work now!
Off with you! Hurry!
All of you, get!
From those new-found shafts
go dig out the gold!
If any be idle,
Mime shall answer.
He'll find it is hard
to escape a whipping!
That I lurk and watch everywhere,
viewless to all,
I fancy Mime knows well!
Loitering still,
just to waste time?
(Draws the ring from his finger, kisses it and holds it out threateningly.)
Fearfully tremble,
you pack of slaves!
Haste for him
who rules the ring.
(Howls and shrieks as the Nibelungs separate —Mime among them—and slip back into their shafts. Alberich watches Wotan and Loge long and mistrustfully.)

ALBERICH

Just what do you want?

WOTAN

We lately heard novel tales
of Nibelhome's mighty land,
dazzling wonders
done here by Alberich,
and eagerness brought us here
to see for ourselves.

ALBERICH

Your envy
drives you to this place.
I think I know that well,
daring guests.

LOGE

Since I am known,
simpleton elf,
then say who am I
that you should snarl!
You shivered once
within a cold hole.
Where were your light
and comforting fire

wenn Loge nie dir gelacht?
Was hülf' dir dein Schmieden,
heizt' ich die Schmiede dir nicht?
Dir bin ich Vetter,
und war dir Freund:
nicht fein drum dünkt mich dein Dank!

ALBERICH

Den Lichtalben
lacht jetzt Loge,
der listige Schelm:
bist du Falscher ihr Freund,
wie mir Freund du einst warst:
haha! mich freut's!
Von ihnen fürcht' ich dann nichts.

LOGE

So denk' ich, kannst du mir trau'n?

ALBERICH

Deiner Untreu trau' ich,
nicht deiner Treu'! —
(Eine herausfordernde Stellung annehmend.)
Doch getrost trotz' ich euch allen.

LOGE

Hohen Mut
verleiht deine Macht;
grimmig gross
wuchs dir die Kraft!

ALBERICH

Siehst du den Hort,
den mein Heer
dort mir gehäuft?

LOGE

So neidlichen sah ich noch nie

ALBERICH

Das ist für heut',
ein kärglich Häufchen!
Kühn und mächtig
soll er künftig sich mehren.

WOTAN

Zu was doch frommt dir der Hort,
da freudlos Nibelheim,
und nichts für Schätze hier feil?

ALBERICH

Schätze zu schaffen
und Schätze zu bergen,
nützt mir Nibelheims Nacht.
Doch mit dem Hort,
in der Höhle gehäuft,
denk' ich dann Wunder zu wirken:
die ganze Welt
gewinn' ich mit ihm mir zu eigen!

WOTAN

Wie beginnst du, Gütiger, das?

ALBERICH

Die in linder Lüfte Weh'n
da oben ihr lebt,
lacht und liebt:
mit goldner Faust
euch Göttliche fang' ich mir alle!
Wie ich der Liebe abgesagt,
alles, was lebt,
soll ihr entsagen!
Mit Golde gekirrt,
nach Gold nur sollt ihr noch gieren!
Auf wonnigen Höh'n,
in seligem Weben
wiegt ihr euch;
den Schwarzalben
verachtet ihr ewigen Schwelger!
Habt Acht! Habt Acht!
Denn dient ihr Männer
erst meiner Macht,
eure schmucken Frau'n,
die mein Frei'n verschmäht,
sie zwingt zur Lust sich der Zwerg,
lacht Liebe ihm nicht!
(Wild lachend.)
Ha ha ha ha!
Habt ihr's gehört?
Habt acht!
Habt acht vor dem nächtlichen Heer,
entsteigt des Niblungen Hort
aus stummer Tiefe zu Tag!

WOTAN
(auffahrend)

Vergeh', frevelnder Gauch!

ALBERICH

Was sagt der?

LOGE
(ist dazwischengetreten)

Sei doch bei Sinnen!
(Zu Alberich.)
Wen doch fasste nicht Wunder,
erfährt er Alberichs Werk?
Gelingt deiner herrlichen List,
was mit dem Horte du heischest:
den Mächtigsten muss ich dich rühmen;

if Loge had not been there,
and where were your forging
had I not heated the forge?
Though I'm your cousin
and was your friend,
I don't think much of your thanks!

ALBERICH

You smile now,
on light-elves, Loge,
you cunning rogue!
Are you, false one, their friend,
as you once were my own?
Ha ha! That's fine,
I need not fear them at all.

LOGE

I think I'm worthy your trust.

ALBERICH

I can trust your untruth but not
    your truth!
I'm secure,
and I defy you!

LOGE

It's your might
has made you so bold.
Grimly great
waxes your strength!

ALBERICH

Look at the hoard
which my host piled in a heap.

LOGE

I never have seen one so fine.

ALBERICH

That's for today
the merest trifle!
Bravely towering it will grow in the
    future!

WOTAN

But what's your use for the hoard
in joyless Nibelhome
where nothing's bought with such wealth?

ALBERICH

Treasures to garner
and treasures to bury,
so serves Nibelhome's might.
But with the hoard
that is heaped high in caves
watch for the wonder I'm planning:
the gold I gain
will win me rule of this planet.

WOTAN

How, my good man, can you do that?

ALBERICH

You who, lapped in balmy airs,
up there above live,
laugh and love:
my golden grip
shall totter you gods to your downfall!
As I have forsworn love for good,
all things that live,
too, shall forswear it!
Ensnared by my gold,
just gold alone shall you long for!
On glorious heights,
in exquisite raptures
rock yourselves!
The elves meet your scorn,
you reveling immortals!
Take care!
take care!
For when you men
first serve my commands,
then your proud-decked women
with their scorn for my love
shall serve my pleasure at will,
though love shall be out!
                    (*laughing wildly*)

Ha ha ha ha!
Have I been heard?
Beware!
Beware of the armies of night,
when the Nibelung hoard shall arise
from silent darkness—to day!

WOTAN
(*starting*)

Away, rascally wretch!

ALBERICH

What says he?

LOGE

Back to your senses!
Who can keep back his wonder
when seeing Alberich's work?
If what you have planned with the hoard
prospers through masterly cunning,
I surely must hail you as mightiest;

denn Mond und Stern',
und die strahlende Sonne,
sie auch dürfen nicht anders,
dienen müssen sie dir.
Doch — wichtig acht' ich vor allem,
dass des Hortes Häufer,
der Niblungen Heer,
neidlos dir geneigt.
Einen Reif rührtest du kühn;
dem zagte zitternd dein Volk: —
doch, wenn im Schlaf
ein Dieb dich beschlich,
den Ring schlau dir entriss, —
wie wahrtest du, Weiser, dich dann?

ALBERICH

Der Listigste dünkt sich Loge;
andre denkt er
immer sich dumm:
dass sein ich bedürfte
zu Rat und Dienst,
um harten Dank,
das hörte der Dieb jetzt gern!
Den hehlenden Helm
ersann ich mir selbst;
der sorglichste Schmied,
Mime musst' ihn mir schmieden:
schnell mich zu wandeln,
nach meinem Wunsch
die Gestalt mir zu tauschen,
taugt der Helm.
Niemand sieht mich,
wenn er mich sucht;
doch überall bin ich,
geborgen dem Blick.
So ohne Sorge
bin ich selbst sicher vor dir,
du fromm sorgender Freund!

LOGE

Vieles sah ich,
Seltsames fand ich,
doch solches Wunder
gewahrt' ich nie.
Dem Werk ohnegleichen
kann ich nicht glauben;
wäre dies eine möglich,
deine Macht währte dann ewig!

ALBERICH

Meinst du, ich lüg'
und prahle wie Loge?

LOGE

Bis ich's geprüft,
bezweifl' ich, Zwerg, dein Wort.

ALBERICH

Vor Klugheit bläht sich
zum platzen der Blöde:
nun plage dich Neid!
Bestimm', in welcher Gestalt
soll ich jach vor dir stehn?

LOGE

In welcher du willst:
nur mach' vor Staunen mich stumm!

ALBERICH
(hat den Helm aufgesetzt)

"Riesenwurm
winde sich ringelnd!"
(Sogleich verschwindet er: eine ungeheure Riesenschlange windet sich statt seiner am Boden; sie bäumt sich und streckt den aufgesperrten Rachen nach Wotan und Loge hin.)

LOGE
(stellt sich von Furcht ergriffen)

Ohe!

WOTAN

Ha ha ha!
Gut, Alberich!

LOGE

Schreckliche . . .
. . . Schlange, verschlinge mich nicht!
Schone . . .
. . . Logen das Leben!

WOTAN

Gut, du Arger! . . .
. . . Wie wuchs so rasch
zum riesigen Wurme der Zwerg!

(Die Schlange verschwindet; statt ihrer erscheint sogleich Alberich wieder in seiner wirklichen Gestalt.)

ALBERICH

Hehe! ihr Klugen!
glaubt ihr mir nun?

LOGE

Mein Zittern mag dir's bezeugen!
Zur grossen Schlange
schufst du dich schnell:
weil ich's gewahrt,

for moon and stars,
and the sun in his glory,
even they must accept you—
also serve you as thralls.
Yet, let me warn you to keep
all of your Nibelung heapers
of gold in a state
free from servile hate.
You have deft touch of your ring:
your people tremble with fear.
Yet if a thief
slipped in while you slept,
and then pulled off your ring,
what, wise one, would come of your plans?

ALBERICH

He thinks himself sharp and clever,
but he deems
all others are fools!
He hopes I am needing
aid and advice—
on iron terms.
The thief would enjoy the thought!
The helmet that hides
was planned by myself.
The cunningest smith,
Mime, forged it to order.
Fast it transforms me
just as I wish
to a form that is different.
Thus the helm.
No one sees me,
much as he tries.
Yet, though I am hidden,
I still can perform.
I am free from care,
and safe even from you,
my fine, provident friend!

LOGE

Much I've looked at,
some of it wondrous,
but have not witnessed
a thing like this.
This work without equal
sounds like a fable.
If this can really happen,
then your might's truly quite boundless!

ALBERICH

Think you I lie
and prattle like Loge?

LOGE

Till it is proved,
friend dwarf, I doubt your word.

ALBERICH

Your cunning, blockhead,
has filled you to bursting.
Now, plague on your spite.
Decide right here on the shape
you would like me to take.

LOGE

Whatever you will,
but make me mute with amaze!

ALBERICH
(putting on the Tarnhelm)

"Giant snake,
coiling and winding!"

(He instantly disappears and in his place
writhes a monstrous serpent on the ground.
It rears and opens its outstretched jaws at
Wotan and Loge.)

LOGE
(pretending fear)

Ohe! Ohe!

WOTAN
(laughing)

Ha ha ha! Ha ha ha!
Good, Alberich!

LOGE

Horrible serpent,
don't swallow me up!
Spare the life of poor Loge!

WOTAN

Good, you rascal!
How fast the dwarf
has grown to a dragonish foe!
(The serpent disappears and Alberich reappears in his natural form.)

ALBERICH

Ha ha! you smart ones!
Now do you know?

LOGE
(his voice quavering)

My trembling, surely, should prove it!
You made the monstrous
serpent with speed!
Now that I've seen,

willig glaub' ich dem Wunder.
Doch, wie du wuchsest,
kannst du auch winzig
und klein dich schaffen?
Das Klügste schien' mir das,
Gefahren schlau zu entflieh'n:
das aber dünkt mich zu schwer.

ALBERICH

Zu schwer dir,
weil du zu dumm!
Wie klein soll ich sein?

LOGE

Dass die feinste Klinze dich fasse,
wo bang die Kröte sich birgt.

ALBERICH

Pah! nichts leichter!
Luge du her!
(Er setzt den Tarnhelm wieder auf.)
"Krumm und grau
krieche Kröte!"
(Er verschwindet; die Götter gewahren im Gestein
eine Kröte auf sich zukriechen.)

LOGE
(zu Wotan)

Dort die Kröte!
Greife sie rasch!
(Wotan setzt seinen Fuß auf die Kröte, Loge fährt
ihr nach dem Kopfe und hält den Tarnhelm in der
Hand.)

ALBERICH
(wird plötzlich in seiner wirklichen Gestalt
sichtbar, wie er sich unter Wotans Füße windet)

Ohe! Verflucht!
Ich bin gefangen!

LOGE

Halt' ihn fest,
bis ich ihn band.
(Er hat ein Bastseil hervorgeholt und bindet Alberich damit Hände und Beine, den Geknebelten,
der sich wütend zu wehren sucht, fassen dann beide und schleppen ihn mit sich nach der Kluft, aus
der sie herabkamen.)

Nur schnell hinauf!
dort ist er unser!
(Sie verschwinden, aufwärts steigend.)

4. SZENE

*Die Szene verwandelt sich, nur in umgekehrter
Weise, wie zuvor; die Verwandlung führt wieder
an den Schmieden vorüber. Fortdauernde Verwandlung nach oben. Schließlich erscheint wieder die*

freie Gegend auf Bergeshöhen

*wie in der zweiten Szene nur ist sie jetzt noch in
fahle Nebel verhüllt.*

LOGE

Da, Vetter,
sitze du fest!
Luge, Liebster,
dort liegt die Welt,
die du Lung'rer gewinnen dir willst:
welch Stellchen, sag',
bestimmst du drin mir zum Stall?
(Er schlägt ihm tanzend Schnippchen.)

ALBERICH

Schändlicher Schächer!
Du Schalk! Du Schelm!
Löse den Bast,
binde mich los;
den Frevel sonst büssest du Frecher!

WOTAN

Gefangen bist du,
fest mir gefesselt,
wie du die Welt,
was lebt and webt,
in deiner Gewalt schon wähntest;
in Banden liegst du vor mir,
du Banger kannst es nicht leugnen!
Zu ledigen dich,
bedarf's nun der Lösung.

ALBERICH

O ich Tropf!
ich träumender Tor!
Wie dumm traut' ich
dem diebischen Trug!
Furchtbare Rache
räche den Fehl!

LOGE

Soll Rache dir frommen,
vor allem rate dich frei:
dem gebund'nen Manne
büsst kein Freier den Frevel.
Drum sinnst du auf Rache
rasch ohne Säumen
sorg' um die Lösung zunächst!
(Er zeigt ihm. mit den Fingern schnalzend, die Art
der Lösung an.)

ALBERICH

So heischt, was ihr begehrt!

I confess to the wonder.
Since you grew greater,
can you grow smaller
and be quite tiny?
The smartest way, I think,
to hide from dangerous foes.
But maybe that is too hard.

ALBERICH

Too hard? Yes,
if you are dumb!
How small shall I be?

LOGE

That the smallest crack may contain you—
a size just right for a toad.

ALBERICH

Pah! Quite easy! Look at me now!
(He puts on the helmet.)
"Creeping toad,
gray and crooked!"
(He vanishes, and a toad is seen crawling on the rocks.)

LOGE
(to Wotan)

There! He did it!
Capture him, quick!
(Wotan sets his foot on the toad. Loge puts his hand to its head and seizes the Tarnhelm.)

ALBERICH

Oho! Accurst!
Now they have caught me!

LOGE

Hold him fast,
till he is bound!
(Alberich suddenly becomes visible in his own shape, writhing under Wotan's foot.)

(binding him with bast rope)

Up we go fast!
There we shall hold him!

(The prisoner, though trying furiously to escape, is dragged by both to the shaft from which they descended. There they disappear, mounting upward. The scene now changes again, but in the reverse direction. Anvils are heard until we reach the upper regions. There Wotan and Loge, with the pinioned Alberich mount from the cleft.)

SCENE 4

An Open Space on the Mountain Heights
(A pale mist shrouds all.)

LOGE

There, kinsman,
take a seat here!
Look, beloved,
there lies the world
which the lazybones wishes to rule.
What corner, pray,
is set aside for my stall?
(He dances around him, snapping his fingers.)

ALBERICH

Scandalous schemer!
You rogue! You thief!
Loosen the rope!
Get me untied!
Or, villain, you'll surely regret it!

WOTAN

You're really caught now,
fast in my fetters,
just when you dreamed
that all that lived
were ready to be your servants.
You lie now, bound at my feet.
You cannot, trembler, deny it.
To let you go free
we must have a ransom.

ALBERICH

I'm a dolt,
a fool in a dream
to have faith
in such treacherous tricks!
Fearful revenge
shall pay for my fault!

LOGE

For vengeance to help you,
you first must talk yourself free!
To a fettered man
no free man answers for outrage.
So, since you want vengeance,
swift, that delays not,
think of the ransom we ask.
(He snaps his fingers, indicating the kind of ransom.)

ALBERICH

Then state, what are your terms?

DAS RHEINGOLD

WOTAN

Den Hort und dein helles Gold.

ALBERICH

Gieriges Gaunergezücht!

(Für sich.)

Doch behalt' ich mir nur den Ring,
des Hortes entrat' ich dann leicht;
denn von neuem gewonnen
und wonnig genährt
ist er bald durch des Ringes Gebot:
eine Witzigung wär's,
die weise mich macht;
zu teuer nicht zahl' ich die Zucht,
lass' für die Lehre ich den Tand.

WOTAN

Erlegst du den Hort?

ALBERICH

Löst mir die Hand,
so ruf' ich ihn her.

(Loge löst ihm die Schlinge an der rechten Hand. Alberich berührt den Ring mit den Lippen und murmelt heimlich einen Befehl.)

Wohlan, die Niblungen
rief ich mir nah.
Ihrem Herrn gehorchend,
hör' ich den Hort
aus der Tiefe sie führen zu Tag:
nun löst mich vom lästigen Band

WOTAN

Nicht eh'r, bis alles gezahlt.

(Die Nibelungen steigen aus der Kluft herauf, mit den Geschmeiden des Hortes beladen. Während des Folgen den schichten sie den Hort auf.)

ALBERICH

O schändliche Schmach!
dass die scheuen Knechte
geknebelt selbst mich erschau'n!

(Zu den Nibelungen.)

Dorthin geführt,
wie ich's befehl'!
All zuhauf
schichtet den Hort!
Helf' ich euch Lahmen?
Hierher nicht gelugt!
Rasch da! rasch!
Dann rührt euch von hinnen,
dass ihr mir schafft!
Fort in die Schachten!

Weh' euch, treff' ich euch faul!
Auf den Fersen folg' ich euch nach!

(Er küßt seinen Ring und streckt ihn gebieterisch aus. Wie von einem Schlage getroffen, drängen sich die Nibelungen scheu und ängstlich der Kluft zu, in die sie schnell hinabschlüpfen.)

Gezahlt hab' ich;
nun lass' mich zieh'n!
Und das Helmgeschmeid',
das Loge dort hält,
das gebt mir nun gütlich zurück!

LOGE

(den Tarnhelm zum Horte werfend)

Zur Busse gehört auch die Beute.

ALBERICH

Verfluchter Dieb!

(Leise.)

Doch nur Geduld!
Der den alten mir schuf,
schafft einen andern:
noch halt' ich die Macht,
der Mime gehorcht.
Schlimm zwar ist's,
dem schlauen Feind
zu lassen die listige Wehr!
Nun denn! Alberich
liess euch alles:
jetzt löst, ihr Bösen, das Band!

LOGE

(zu Wotan)

Bist du befriedigt?
lass' ich ihn frei?

WOTAN

(entsetzt)

Ein goldner Ring
ragt dir am Finger:
hörst du, Alp?
der, acht' ich, gehört mit zum Hort.
Zu deiner Lösung
musst du ihn lassen.

ALBERICH

(bebend)

Der Ring?
Das Leben — doch nicht den Ring!

WOTAN

(heftiger)

Den Reif' verlang' ich:
mit dem Leben mach', was du willst!

WOTAN

The hoard and your gleaming gold.

ALBERICH

Greedy and criminal crew!
(aside)
If I still have the magic ring
I freely may give them the hoard,
for I soon will be able to build one anew,
through the magical might of the ring.
Here's a lesson, I think,
that sharpens my wit.
I think I'm getting off cheap,
losing a toy and nothing else.

WOTAN

Now what of the hoard?

ALBERICH

Loosen my hand,
I'll have it brought in.
(Loge unties his right hand. Alberich puts the ring to his lips and murmurs a secret spell.)
All right! The Nibelungs
will come at my call!
They obey my orders.
Mark how they march
from the depths to the day with the hoard.
Now loosen these burdensome bonds!

WOTAN

No use, till all has been paid.

(The Nibelungs ascend from the cleft, laden with the treasures of the hoard, which they start to pile up.)

ALBERICH

O, shameful disgrace,
that my timid varlets
should view me shackled like this.
(to the Nibelungs)

Carry it there
as I command!
Make a pile!
Heap it up high!
Need any help there?
But don't look this way!
Quick there! Quick!
Then hurry and leave us!
Off to your jobs!
Back to your mine pits!
Woe to laggards at work!
I shall follow close at your heels!

(He kisses his ring and stretches it out commandingly. As if struck by a blow the Nibelungs rush in fear and terror to the cleft, into which they slip.)

I've paid fully,
now let me leave.
And the smithied helm
that Loge has there,
be good now and give it back!

LOGE
(throwing the Tarnhelm upon the hoard)
We take it as part of the booty.

ALBERICH

Accursed thief!
Yet wait a while!
He who forged me the first,
let him repeat it.
I still hold the might
that Mime obeys.
Bad indeed
to yield my foes
weapons I need for defense!
Now then, everything
has been given.
Now loose—you bad men—my bonds.

LOGE

Are you contented?
Should he be freed?

WOTAN

A golden ring
shows on your finger.
Hear me, elf.
That also belongs with the hoard.
To get your freedom,
that must be left us.

ALBERICH
(stunned)

The ring?
My life then, but not the ring.

WOTAN
(more violently)
I ask the ring too:
with your life just do as you please.

ALBERICH

Lös' ich mir Leib und Leben,
den Ring auch muss ich mir lösen;
Hand und Haupt,
Aug' und Ohr
sind nicht mehr mein Eigen,
als hier dieser rote Ring!

WOTAN

Dein Eigen nennst du den Ring?
Rasest du, schamloser Albe?
Nüchtern sag',
wem entnahmst du das Gold,
daraus du den schimmernden schufst?
War's dein Eigen,
was du Arger
der Wassertiefe entwandt?
Bei des Rheines Töchtern hole dir Rat,
ob ihr Gold sie
zu eigen dir gaben,
das du zum Ring dir geraubt!

ALBERICH

Schmähliche Tücke!
Schändlicher Trug!
Wirfst du Schächer
die Schuld mir vor,
die dir so wonnig erwünscht?
Wie gern raubtest
du selbst dem Rheine das Gold,
war nur so leicht
die Kunst, es zu schmieden, erlangt?
Wie glückt es nun
dir Gleissner zum Heil,
dass der Niblung, ich,
aus schmählicher Not,
in des Zornes Zwange,
den schrecklichen Zauber gewann,
dess' Werk nun lustig dir lacht!
Des Unseligen,
Angstversehrten
fluchfertige,
furchtbare Tat,
zu fürstlichem Tand
soll sie fröhlich dir taugen?
zur Freude dir frommen mein Fluch? —
Hüte dich,
herrischer Gott!
Frevelte ich,
so frevelt' ich frei an mir:

doch an allem, was war,
ist und wird,
frevelst, Ewiger, du,
entreissest du frech mir den Ring!

WOTAN

Her den Ring!
Kein Recht an ihm
schwörst du schwatzend dir zu.
*(Er ergreift Alberich und entzieht seinem
Finger mit heftiger Gewalt den Ring.)*

ALBERICH
(gräßlich aufschreiend)

Ha! Zertrümmert! Zerknickt!
Der Traurigen traurigster Knecht!

WOTAN
(den Ring betrachtend)

Nun halt' ich, was mich erhebt,
der Mächtigen mächtigsten Herrn!
(Er steckt den Ring an.)

LOGE
(zu Wotan)

Ist er gelöst?

WOTAN

Bind' ihn los!

LOGE
(löst Alberich vollends die Bande)

Schlüpfe denn heim!
Keine Schlinge hält dich:
frei fahre dahin!

ALBERICH
(sich vom Boden erhebend)

Bin ich nun frei? Ha, ha!
(Mit wütendem Lachen.)

Wirklich frei? —
So grüss' euch denn
meiner Freiheit erster Gruss! —
Wie durch Fluch er mir geriet,
verflucht sei dieser Ring!
Gab sein Gold
mir Macht ohne Mass,
nun zeug' sein Zauber
Tod dem, der ihn trägt!
Kein Froher soll
seiner sich freu'n,
keinem Glücklichen lache
sein lichter Glanz!

ALBERICH

But if my life is left me,
the ring too must be included.
Hand and head,
eye and ear—
they are mine no more
than this ring that is called my own.

WOTAN

You really call it your own?
Shameless elf, are you not raving?
Simply say
where you borrowed the gold
from which you have welded the ring.
Did you own it
when you took it
from out the depths of the Rhine?
Ask the river maidens
whether they said
that they gave you
their gold for possession
which you have robbed for your ring!

ALBERICH

Shameful malignance!
Scandalous fraud!
Would you, villainy,
blame me for the deed
you dreamt of yourself?
Yourself you would have
gladly stolen the gold,
had it been
just as easy to forge as to steal.
You hypocrite,
how lucky you are
that the Nibelung here,
in shameful despite,
in a wave of wrath,
won the gold with its terrible charm,
whose work now smiles on you fair.
The unhallowed one's
anguish-ridden,
curse-harboring,
terrible deed,
is only a toy
for a prince's amusement.
Shall peace be your prize for my curse?
Guard yourself,
conquering god!
When I do sin,
I sin to myself alone.
But the virtuous god
sins against all
that was, is and will be,
if rashly he seizes my ring!

WOTAN

Yield the ring!
What good is babbling
to prove you are right.
(He seizes Alberich and tears the ring from his fingers.)

ALBERICH
(shrieking horribly)

I'm shattered
and crushed,
the saddest of sorrowful slaves!

WOTAN
(contemplating the ring)

I hold here what sets me up—
the strongest of mightiest lords!
(He puts the ring on.)

LOGE
(to Wotan)

Is he released?

WOTAN

Set him free!
(Loge completely unties Alberich's bonds.)

LOGE
(to Alberich)

Slip away home!
No more fetters bind you!
Fare freely from here!

ALBERICH
(raising himself)

Am I now free?
(with a raging laugh)
Really free?
I greet you then
with my freedom's first salute!
As the ring came as a curse,
so cursed be it now!
Through its gold
came measureless might,
now let its lords
find measureless death.
Let none rejoice,
owning the ring.
Let no gleam from it
shine on a happy mind!

Wer ihn besitzt,
den sehre die Sorge,
und wer ihn nicht hat,
den Nage der Neid!
Jeder giere
nach seinem Gut,
doch keiner geniesse
mit Nutzen sein!
Ohne Wucher hüt' ihn sein Herr;
doch den Würger zieh' er ihm zu!
Dem Tode verfallen,
fessle den Feigen die Furcht:
solang er lebt,
sterb' er lechzend dahin,
des Ringes Herr
als des Ringes Knecht:
bis in meiner Hand
den geraubten wieder ich halte! —
So segnet
in höchster Not
der Nibelung seinen Ring!
Behalt' ihn nun,
(Lachend.)
hüte ihn wohl:
(Grimmig.)
meinem Fluch fliehest du nicht!
(Er verschwindet schnell in der Kluft. Der dichte Nebel auft des Vordergrundes klärt sich allmählich auf.)

LOGE

Lauschtest du
seinem Liebesgruss?

WOTAN
(in den Anblick des Ringes an seiner Hand versunken).

Gönn' ihm die geifernde Lust!
(Es wird immer heller.)

LOGE
(nach rechts in die Szene blickend)

Fasolt und Fafner
nahen von fern:
Freia führen sie her.
(Aus dem sich immer mehr zerteilenden Nebel erscheinen Donner, Froh und Fricka und eilen dem Vordergrunde zu.)

FROH

Sie kehrten zurück!

DONNER

Willkommen, Bruder!

FRICKA
(besorgt zu Wotan)

Bringst du gute Kunde?

LOGE
(auf den Hort deutend)

Mit List und Gewalt
gelang das Werk:
dort liegt, was Freia löst.

DONNER

Aus der Riesen Haft
naht dort die Holde.

FROH

Wie liebliche Luft
wieder uns weht,
wonnig' Gefühl
die Sinne erfüllt!
Traurig ging es uns allen,
getrennt für immer von ihr,
die leidlos ewiger Jugend
jubelnde Lust uns verleiht.

(Der Vordergrund ist wieder hell geworden; das Aussehen der Götter gewinnt wieder die erste Frische: über dem Hintergrunde haftet jedoch noch der Nebelschleier, so daß die Burg unsichtbar bleibt. Fasolt und Fafner treten auf, Freia zwischen sich führend.)

FRICKA
(eilt freudig auf die Schwester zu, um sie zu umarmen)

Lieblichste Schwester,
süsseste Lust!
bist du mir wiedergewonnen?

FASOLT
(ihr wehrend)

Halt! Nicht sie berührt!
Noch gehört sie uns.
Auf Riesenheims
ragender Mark
rasteten wir;
mit treuem Mut
des Vertrages Pfand
pflegten wir.
So sehr mich's reut,
zurück doch bring' ich's,
erlegt uns Brüdern
die Lösung ihr.

WOTAN

Bereit liegt die Lösung:
des Goldes Mass
sei nun gütlich gemessen.

FASOLT

Das Weib zu missen,
wisse, gemutet mich weh:

Care shall consume
the ones who possess it,
and envy gnaw those
who wish that they did!
Each shall lust
after its delights,
yet no one shall find
any profit there!
Let its owner never be blest,
Let it draw the slayer to his doom!
Let death be his portion,
fear be the bread that he eats!
And while he lives,
let him long for his death—
this treasure's lord
as the treasure's slave,
till I hold again
in my hand the ring I was robbed of!
Thus, urged by
the sorest of spite,
the Nibelung blesses his ring.
So keep it now,
(laughing)
guard it with care!
(wrathfully)
But you can't flee from my curse!
(He disappears into the cleft. The thick vapor gradually clears off.)

LOGE

Did you mark
all his words of love?

WOTAN
(absorbed in contemplation of the ring)
Grant him the joy of complaint!
(It continues to get lighter.)

LOGE
(looking into the distance)
Fasolt and Fafner soon will be here.
Freia follows them here.
(Out of the still dispersing mist emerge Donner, Froh and Fricka.)

FROH

They're on their way back!

DONNER

You're welcome, brother!

FRICKA
(anxiously to Wotan)
Have you brought good tidings?

LOGE
(pointing to the hoard)
With cunning and force
we did the work.
Right there lies Freia's price.

DONNER

See the fair one come,
free of the giants.

FROH

How lovely the air
wafting again!
Feelings of joy
are filling our thoughts!
Think of how we would suffer,
forever parted from her
who lends us life without sorrow,
youth that is endless in joy.
(Fasolt and Fafner enter, leading Freia between them. Fricka hastens joyfully toward her sister. The gods appear restored in aspect. In the background, however, there still hovers a veil of mist, keeping the distant castle invisible.)

FRICKA

Loveliest sister!
Sweetest delight!
Have you returned as our ransom?

FASOLT
(stopping her)
Halt! Hold off a while!
Freia still is ours.
We rested some,
there on the ridge,
Gianthome's mark.
We took best care
of our bargain's pledge,
treating her fair,
I've brought her back,
but much regret this.
Now pay us brothers
the ransom due.

WOTAN

Right there lies the ransom.
The golden mass
must be fittingly measured.

FASOLT

To lose this maiden
really will sadden my heart.

soll aus dem Sinn sie mir schwinden,
des Geschmeides Hort
häufet denn so,
dass meinem Blick
die Blühende ganz er verdeck'!

WOTAN

So stellt das Mass
nach Freia's Gestalt.
(Freia wird von den beiden Riesen in die Mitte gestellt. Darauf stoßen sie ihre Pfähle zu Freias beiden Seiten so in den Boden, daß sie gleiche Höhe und Breite mit ihrer Gestalt messen.)

FAFNER

Gepflanzt sind die Pfähle
nach Pfandes Mass:
gehäuft nun füll' es der Hort.

WOTAN

Eilt mit dem Werk:
widerlich ist mir's!

LOGE

Hilf mir, Froh!

FROH

Freias Schmach
eil' ich zu enden.
(Loge und Froh häufen hastig zwischen den Pfählen die Geschmeide.)

FAFNER

Nicht so leicht
und locker gefügt!
(Er drückt mit roher Kraft die Geschmeide dicht zusammen.)
Fest und dicht
füll' er das Mass!
(Er beugt sich, um nach Lücken zu spähen.)
Hier lug' ich noch durch:
verstopft mir die Lücken!

LOGE

Zurück, du Grober!

FAFNER

Hierher!

LOGE

Greif' mir nichts an!

FAFNER

Hierher! die Klinze verklemmt!

WOTAN
(unmutig sich abwendend)

Tief in der Brust
brennt mir die Schmach!

FRICKA
(den Blick auf Freia geheftet)

Sieh, wie in Schmach
schmählich die Edle steht:
um Erlösung fleht
stumm der leidende Blick.
Böser Mann!
der Minnigen botest du das!

FAFNER

Noch mehr! Noch mehr hieher!

DONNER

Kaum halt' ich mich:
schäumende Wut
weckt mir der schamlose Wicht!
Hierher, du Hund!
willst du messen,
so miss dich selber mit mir!

FAFNER

Ruhig, Donner!
Rolle, wo's taugt:
hier nützt dein Rasseln dir nichts!

DONNER
(holt aus)

Nicht dich Schmähl'chen zu zerschmettern?

WOTAN

Friede doch!
Schon dünkt mich Freia verdeckt.

LOGE

Der Hort ging auf.

FAFNER
(mißt den Hort genau mit dem Blick und späht nach Lücken)

Noch schimmert mir Holdas Haar:
dort das Gewirk
wirf auf den Hort!

LOGE

Wie? auch den Helm?

FAFNER

Hurtig, her mit ihm!

But there's a way to forget her:
pile the treasure hoard
high in a heap,
so as to cover
all of the fair one from me.

WOTAN

Then place the girl
as gauge for the heap!

(The two giants set Freia in the middle. Then they thrust their staves into the ground on each side of her, so as to measure her height and breadth.)

FAFNER

Our staves have been planted
to gauge her form.
Now heap the hoard to this height.

WOTAN

Haste with the work.
Really distasteful!

LOGE

Help me, Froh!

FROH

I must end
Freia's dishonor.
(Loge and Froh heap up the treasure between the staves.)

FAFNER

Not so light
and loose with this heap!
(He roughly presses the ornaments closer together.)
Tight and close, fill up the gauge!
(He looks for crevices.)
I still can see through,
so fill in the openings!

LOGE

Get back, you lubber!

FAFNER

Come here!

LOGE

Leave it alone!

FAFNER

Come here!
This chink must be closed!

WOTAN
(turning away, downcast)

Deep is the shame
burning my breast!

FRICKA

Deep is the shame,
there where the fair one stands!
And she hopes for help,
mute, with sorrowful gaze!
Wicked man!
It's you brought our dear one to this!

FAFNER

Still more! Still more this way!

DONNER

This is too much!
Shameless, this rogue
wakens my ravening rage.
Come here, you dog!
Must you measure,
then match yourself against me!

FAFNER

Calmly, Donner!
Not so much noise!
We need no rumblings from you.

DONNER
(aiming a blow)

Not to shake you to pieces?

WOTAN

Be at peace!
I think she's covered by now.

LOGE
(watching Fafner measure the hoard critically)

The hoard gives out!

FAFNER

The sheen of her hair still shows.
Toss on that trinket
with the rest.

LOGE

What? Even the helm?

FAFNER

Quickly! Here with it!

DAS RHEINGOLD

WOTAN

Lass ihn denn fahren!

LOGE
(wirft den Tarnhelm auf den Hort)

So sind wir denn fertig!
Seid ihr zufrieden?

FASOLT

Freia, die Schöne,
schau' ich nicht mehr:
so ist sie gelöst?
muss ich sie lassen?
(Er tritt nahe hinzu und späht durch den Hort.)
Weh'! noch blitzt
ihr Blick zu mir her;
des Auges Stern
strahlt mich noch an;
durch eine Spalte
muss ich's erspähn.
(Außer sich.)
Seh' ich dies wonnige Auge,
von dem Weibe lass' ich nicht ab!

FAFNER

He! euch rat' ich,
verstopft mir die Ritze!

LOGE

Nimmersatte!
seht ihr denn nicht,
ganz schwand uns der Hort?

FAFNER

Mit nichten, Freund!
An Wotans Finger
glänzt von Gold noch ein Ring:
den gebt, die Ritze zu füllen!

WOTAN

Wie? diesen Ring?

LOGE

Lasst euch raten!
Den Rheintöchtern
gehört dies Gold;
ihnen gibt Wotan es wieder.

WOTAN

Was schwatzest du da?
Was schwer ich mir erbeutet,
ohne Bangen wahr' ich's für mich!

LOGE

Schlimm dann steht's
um mein Versprechen,
das ich den Klagenden gab.

WOTAN

Dein Versprechen bindet mich nicht;
als Beute bleibt mir der Reif.

FAFNER

Doch hier zur Lösung
musst du ihn legen.

WOTAN

Fordert frech, was ihr wollt,
alles gewähr' ich;
um alle Welt doch
nicht fahren lass' ich den Ring!

FASOLT
(zieht wütend Freia hinter dem Horte hervor)

Aus dann ist's!
beim Alten bleibt's;
nun folgt uns Freia für immer!

FREIA

Hilfe! Hilfe!

FRICKA

Harter Gott,
gib ihnen nach!

FROH

Spare das Gold nicht!

DONNER

Spende den Ring doch!
(Fafner hält den fortdrängenden Fasolt noch auf;
alle stehen bestürzt.)

WOTAN

Lasst mich in Ruh':
den Reif geb' ich nicht.
(Wotan wendet sich zürnend zur Seite. Die Bühne hat sich von neuem verfinstert; aus der Felskluft zur Seite bricht ein bläulicher Schein hervor: in ihm wird plötzlich Erda sichtbar, die bis zu halber Leibeshöhe aus der Tiefe aufsteigt, sie ist von edler Gestalt, weithin von schwarzem Haar umwallt. Sie streckt die Hand mahnend gegen Wotan aus.)

WOTAN

Let it go also!
(Loge throws it on the heap.)

LOGE

So now we are ready!
Anything further?

FASOLT

Freia, the radiant,
passes from sight.
I see she's redeemed.
Must I now leave her?

(He goes up to the hoard and peeps through it.)

Ah! Her glance
yet gleams on me here.
Her starry eyes
dazzle my own.
I still can spy them
right through this space.
(excited)
And I can't part from this woman
while I see the grace of one eye.

FAFNER

Ha! I warn you
to stop up that cranny!

LOGE

Never sated!
Can you not see
our hoard is all spent!

FAFNER

Not wholly, friend!
On Wotan's finger
gleams a ring made of gold.
Give that to fill up the cranny.

WOTAN

What! Give the ring?

LOGE

Let me tell you,
the Rhine-daughters
must have this gold.
Wotan plans soon to restore it.

WOTAN

What babbling is this?
I sweated for this booty!
I shall keep it fearlessly mine!

LOGE

That means ruin
to the promise
I gave the sorrowing maids!

WOTAN

What you said's not binding to me.
The ring is booty I won.

FAFNER

Now add the final
part of the ransom.

WOTAN

Ask as much as you will,
all will be granted;
but all the world
cannot make me give up the ring.
(Fasolt angrily pulls Freia from behind the hoard.)

FASOLT

All is off!
The old way stands.
We'll keep your Freia forever!

FREIA

Help me! Help me!

FRICKA

Haughty god!
Do as they ask!

FROH

Hold not the gold back!

DONNER

Give them the ring too!
(Fafner holds back Fasolt, who is hurrying away.)

WOTAN

Leave me alone!
The ring stays with me!
(He turns away in wrath.)
(The scene darkens. From the rocky cleft at the side breaks forth a bluish light, in which Erda suddenly becomes visible, rising up to half her height from below. She stretches out a warning hand to Wotan.)

Erda

Weiche, Wotan! weiche!
Flieh' des Ringes Fluch!
Rettungslos
dunklem Verderben
weiht dich sein Gewinn.

Wotan

Wer bist du, mahnendes Weib?

Erda

Wie alles war, weiss ich;
wie alles wird,
wie alles sein wird,
seh' ich auch:
der ew'gen Welt
Ur-Wala,
Erda mahnt deinen Mut.
Drei der Töchter,
ur-erschaff'ne,
gebar mein Schoss;
was ich sehe,
sagen dir nächtlich die Nornen.
Doch höchste Gefahr
führt mich heut'
selbst zu dir her.
Höre! Höre! Höre!
Alles was ist, endet!
Ein düst'rer Tag
dämmert den Göttern:
dir rat' ich, meide den Ring!

(Sie versinkt langsam bis an die Brust, während der bläuliche Schein zu dunkeln beginnt.)

Wotan

Geheimnisshehr
hallt mir dein Wort:
weile, dass mehr ich wisse!

Erda
(im Versinken)

Ich warnte dich;
du weisst genug:
sinn' in Sorg' und Furcht!
(Sie verschwindet gänzlich.)

Wotan

Soll ich sorgen und fürchten,
dich muss ich fassen,
alles erfahren!
(Er will der Verschwindenden in die Kluft nach, um sie zu halten. Froh und Fricka werfen sich ihm entgegen und halten ihn zurück.)

Fricka

Was willst du, Wütender?

Froh

Halt' ein, Wotan!
Scheue die Edle,
achte ihr Wort!
(Wotan starrt sinnend vor sich hin).

Donner
(sich entschlossen zu den Riesen wendend)

Hört, ihr Riesen!
zurück, und harret:
das Gold wird euch gegeben.

Freia

Darf ich es hoffen?
Dünkt euch Holda
wirklich der Lösung wert?
(Alle blicken gespannt auf Wotan; dieser nach tiefem Sinnen zu sich kommend, erfaßt seinen Speer und schwenkt ihn wie zum Zeichen eines mutigen Entschlusses.)

Wotan

Zu mir, Freia!
du bist befreit:
wieder gekauft
kehr' uns die Jugend zurück!
Ihr Riesen, nehmt euren Ring!

(Er wirft den Ring auf den Hort. Die Riesen lassen Freia los; sie eilt freudig auf die Götter zu, die sie abwechselnd längere Zeit in höchster Freude liebkosen.)

(Fafner breitet sogleich einen ungeheuren Sack aus und macht sich über den Hort her, um ihn da hineinzuschichten).

Fasolt
(dem Bruder sich entgegenwerfend)

Halt, du Gieriger!
Gönne mir auch 'was!
Redliche Teilung
taugt uns beiden.

Fafner

Mehr an der Maid als am Gold
lag dir verliebtem Geck;
mit Müh' zum Tausch
vermocht' ich dich Toren.
Ohne zu teilen
hättest du Freia gefreit:
teil' ich den Hort,
billig behalt' ich
die grösste Hälfte für mich!

ERDA

Yield it, Wotan! Yield it!
Flee the cursed ring!
Dark and despairing destruction
marks its owner's end!

WOTAN

Who are you, woman of doom?

ERDA

Great is my lore. Hearken!
All things that were,
all things that happen,
all to be,
are known to me.
Prime-Vala,
Erda, bids you beware.
Three the daughters
born to me
long before earth was.
What I witness,
nightly the Norns tell to Wotan.
But direst of danger
has brought me
to your aid.
Hear me! Hear me! Hear me!
All things that are, perish!
A mournful day
dawns for Valhalla.
I warn you, give up the ring!
(Erda sinks into the earth to her breast, while the bluish glow begins to fade.)

WOTAN

A lofty lore
sounds in your words.
Wait! Let me hear more wisdom!

ERDA
(sinking)

I've warned you well.
You know enough.
Weigh and fear my words!
(She disappears completely. Wotan seeks to follow and stop her. Froh and Fricka throw themselves in his way and hold him back.)

WOTAN

Why this fear and this worry!
I must detain you,
so I'll know all things!

FRICKA

What would you, maniac?

FROH

Take care, Wotan!
Fear what she tells you!
Hark to her words!
(Wotan gazes thoughtfully before him.)

DONNER
(turning to the giants resolutely)

Hear, you giants!
Go back! Just wait there!
The gold, Wotan will give you.

FREIA

Dare I to hope it!
Well, is Holda
worthy the price required?
(All look expectantly toward Wotan. He, rousing himself from deep thought, grasps his spear and brandishes it.)

WOTAN

Then stay, Freia!
I set you free.
Bought back again,
now let our youth be restored!
You giants, here is your ring!
(He throws the ring upon the hoard. The giants release Freia. She hastens joyfully to the gods, who embrace her in turn, for some time, with the greatest delight.)

(Fafner has meanwhile spread out a huge sack, and busies himself over the hoard, preparing to pack it in.)

FASOLT
(to Fafner)

Stop, you greedy rogue!
Give me some also!
Fairly and squarely
both should share it.

FAFNER

Amorous dolt, you prefer
gold to the girl, I see.
I found it hard
to make you exchange it,
when in desire
to woo her
you thought not to share.
Therefore shall I
keep for my portion
the greatest part of the hoard.

DAS RHEINGOLD

FASOLT
Schändlicher du!
Mir diesen Schimpf?
(Zu den Göttern.)
Euch ruf' ich zu Richtern:
teilet nach Recht
uns redlich den Hort!
(Wotan wendet sich verächtlich ab.)

LOGE
Den Hort lass ihn raffen:
halte du nur auf den Ring!

FASOLT
*(stürzt sich auf Fafner, der immerzu
eingesackt hat)*
Zurück! Du Frecher!
mein ist der Ring;
mir blieb er für Freias Blick!
(Er greift hastig nach dem Reif. Sie ringen.)

FAFNER
Fort mit der Faust!
der Ring ist mein!
(Fasolt entreißt Fafner den Ring.)

FASOLT
Ich halt' ihn, mir gehört er!

FAFNER
(mit einem Pfahle nach Fasolt ausholend)
Halt' ihn fest, dass er nicht fall'!
*(Er streckt Fasolt mit einem Streiche zu Boden,
dem Sterbenden entreißt er dann hastig den Ring.)*
Nun blinzle nach Freias Blick!
An den Reif rührst du nicht mehr!
*(Er steckt den Ring in den Sack und rafft dann
gemächlich vollends den Hort ein.)*

WOTAN
(tief erschüttert)
Furchtbar nun
erfind' ich des Fluches Kraft!

LOGE
Was gleicht, Wotan,
wohl deinem Glücke?
Viel erwarb dir
des Ringes Gewinn;
dass er nun dir genommen,
nützt dir noch mehr:
deine Feinde, sieh!
fällen sich selbst
um das Gold, das du vergabst.

WOTAN
Wie doch Bangen mich bindet!
Sorg' und Furcht
fesseln den Sinn:
wie sie zu enden,
lehre mich Erda:
zu ihr muss ich hinab!

FRICKA
(schmeichelnd sich an ihn schmiegend)
Wo weilst du, Wotan?
Winkt dir nicht hold
die hehre Burg,
die des Gebieters
gastlich bergend nun harrt?

WOTAN
(düster)
Mit bösem Zoll
zahlt' ich den Bau!

DONNER
*(auf den Hintergrund deutend, der noch
in Nebel gehüllt ist)*
Schwüles Gedünst
schwebt in der Luft;
lästig ist mir
der trübe Druck!
Das bleiche Gewölk
samml' ich zu blitzendem Wetter,
das fegt den Himmel mir hell!
*(Er besteigt einen hohen Felsstein am Talabhange
und schwingt dort seinen Hammer; Nebel ziehen
sich um ihn zusammen.)*
Heda! Heda! Hedo!
Zu mir, du Gedüft!
ihr Dünste, zu mir!
Donner, der Herr
ruft euch zu Heer!
(Er schwingt den Hammer.)
Auf des Hammers Schwung
schwebet herbei!
Dunstig Gedämpf!
Schwebend Gedüft!
Donner, der Herr,
ruft euch zu Heer!
Heda! Heda! Hedo!
*(Er verschwindet völlig in einer immer finsterer
sich ballenden Gewitterwolke. Man hört Donners
Hammerschlag schwer auf den Felsstein fallen. ein
starker Blitz entfährt der Wolke; ein heftiger Don-
nerschlag folgt. Froh ist mit dem Gewölk ver-
schwunden.)*

FASOLT

Treacherous thief!
Insolent rogue!
(to the gods)
Come, give us your judgment!
See that we fairly
share in the hoard!
(Wotan turns contemptuously away.)

LOGE

Let him take the treasure.
(Fasolt throws himself on Fafner, who is busily packing up.)
Keep for yourself just the ring!

FASOLT

Away! You cheater! Mine is the ring!
I bought it with Freia's glance!
(He snatches hastily at the ring. They struggle. Fasolt wrests the ring from Fafner.)

FAFNER

Off with your fist!
The ring is mine!

FASOLT

I hold it, for I own it!

FAFNER
(hitting out with his staff)

Hold it tight or it may fall!
(With one stroke he fells Fasolt, then wrests the ring from his dying grasp.)
Now blink upon Freia's face!
You shall no more touch the ring!
(He puts it into the sack and then resumes his packing.)

WOTAN
(horrified)

Fearful force
resides in the mighty curse!

LOGE

What luck, Wotan,
happens as your luck?
What you won
was a great achievement.
Now it's taken away though—
that's better yet!
For your foemen, see,
having your gold,
bring about their doom themselves.

WOTAN

Yet a horror enchains me.
Care and fear
fetter my soul.
Erda shall teach me
how I may end it.
I must go to her now!

FRICKA
(approaching him cajolingly)

Why tarry, then, Wotan?
See how your noble
castle gleams,
gladly awaiting
Wotan, lord of its life.

WOTAN
(gloomily)

A dreadful price
paid for that hall!

DONNER
(pointing toward the back, which is still veiled in mist)

Sweltering mist
hangs in the air.
Thick the pressure
of turbid air.
I'll gather the clouds,
bringing the lightning and thunder,
and clear the fog from the sky!

(Donner mounts a high rock by the precipice and there swings his hammer. During the following the mists collect round him.)
He da! He da! He do!
Come hither, you dews!
Come hither, you mists!
Donner, your lord,
calls you to arms!
(He swings his hammer.)
As this hammer swings,
marshal your ranks!
Vaporly damps!
Hovering dews!
Donner, your lord,
calls you to arms!
He da! He da! He do!

(Donner completely disappears in an ever-thickening and darkening thundercloud. His hammer-stroke is heard to fall heavily on the rocks. A vivid lightning flash darts through the cloud. A violent thunderclap follows. Froh has also disappeared in the clouds.)

Donner
(unsichtbar)

Bruder, hieher!
Weise der Brücke den Weg!

(Plötzlich verzieht sich die Wolke; Donner und Froh werden sichtbar: von ihren Füßen aus zieht sich, mit blendendem Leuchten, eine Regenbogenbrücke über das Tal hinüber bis zur Burg, die jetzt, von der Abendsonne beschienen, im hellsten Glanze erstrahlt. Fafner, der neben der Leiche seines Bruders endlich den ganzen Hort eingerafft, hat den ungeheuren Sack auf dem Rücken, während Donners Gewitterzauber die Bühne verlassen.)

Froh
(der der Brücke mit der ausgestreckten Hand den Weg über das Tal angewiesen, zu den Göttern)

Zur Burg führt die Brücke,
leicht, doch fest eurem Fuss:
beschreitet kühn
ihren schrecklosen Pfad!

(Wotan und die andern Götter sind sprachlos in den prächtigen Anblick verloren.)

Wotan

Abendlich strahlt
der Sonne Auge;
in prächtiger Glut
prangt glänzend die Burg.
In des Morgens Scheine
mutig erschimmernd,
lag sie herrenlos,
hehr verlockend vor mir.
Von Morgen bis Abend,
in Müh' und Angst,
nicht wonnig ward sie gewonnen!
Es naht die Nacht:
vor ihrem Neid
biete sie Bergung nun.
So grüss' ich die Burg,
sicher vor Bang und Grau'n!

(Er wendet sich feierlich zu Fricka.)

Folge mir, Frau:
in Walhall wohne mit mir!

Fricka

Was deutet der Name?
Nie, dünkt mich, hört' ich ihn nennen.

Wotan

Was, mächtig der Furcht,
mein Mut mir erfand,
wenn siegend es lebt,
leg' es den Sinn dir dar.

(Er faßt Fricka an der Hand und schreitet mit ihr langsam der Brücke zu; Froh, Freia und Donner folgen.)

Loge
(im Vordergrunde verharrend und den Göttern nachblickend)

Ihrem Ende eilen sie zu,
die so stark im Bestehen sich wähnen.
Fast schäm' ich mich,
mit ihnen zu schaffen;
zur leckenden Lohe
mich wieder zu wandeln,
spür' ich lockende Lust:
sie aufzuzehren,
die einst mich gezähmt,
statt mit den Blinden
blöd zu vergeh'n,
und waren es göttlichste Götter! —
Nicht dumm dünkte mich das!
Bedenken will ich's:
wer weiss, was ich tu'!

(Er geht, um sich den Göttern in nachlässiger Haltung anzuschließen. Aus der Tiefe hört man den Gesang der Rheintöchter heraufschallen.)

Die drei Rheintochter
(in der Tiefe des Tales, unsichtbar)

Rheingold! Rheingold!
Reines Gold!
Wie lauter und hell
leuchtetest hold du uns!
Um dich, du klares,
wir nun klagen;
gebt uns das Gold!
O gebt uns das reine zurück!

Loge
(späht in das Tal hinab)

Des Rheines Kinder
beklagen des Goldes Raub!

Wotan
(im Begriff, den Fuß auf die Brücke zu setzen, hält an und wendet sich um)

Welch' Klagen klingt zu mir her?
Verwünschte Nicker!
Wehre ihrem Geneck!

DONNER
(invisible)

Brother, come here!
Show us the way to the bridge!
(Suddenly the clouds disperse. Donner and Froh become visible. From their feet stretches in blinding radiance a rainbow-bridge over the valley to the castle, which now gleams in the light of the setting sun.)

FROH
(pointing to the bridge with his outstretched hand, as the way over the valley.)

This bridge to the castle
light, yet firm underfoot,
may now be trod
with a step free of fear!
(Wotan and the other gods are speechless with astonishment at the glorious sight.)

WOTAN

As it sets,
sun's bright eye is glowing.
Its glorious gleam
gilds tower and wall.
In the radiant dawn
it shimmered so bravely,
lying masterless,
nobly greeting its lord.
From morning till evening,
through toil and care,
and not through joy, grew its portals.
The night is nigh.
Against its spite,
friendly our shelter looms.
So, hail to our home,
refuge from fear and dread!
(He turns solemnly to Fricka.)
Follow me, wife!
Let Valhall harbor us both.

FRICKA

Just what is this Valhall!
I've never heard you once name it!

WOTAN

The fort I have found
to finish all fear,
if born to success,
soon will explain its name.

(He grasps Fricka by the hand and paces with her slowly toward the bridge. Froh, Freia and Donner follow.)

LOGE
(remaining behind)

Now behold them haste to their end,
while they fancy their being immortal!
I feel ashamed
to share in their actions.
A burning temptation
to flare into blazes
builds a wish in my heart
to burn those up
who had once made me tame,
rather than blindly
die with the blind
although they are gods the most godlike!
I think that is the thing!
I'll give it some thought.
Who knows what I'll do?
(He goes up with assumed carelessness to join the gods. The three Rhine maidens are heard below in the valley, invisible.)

RHINE MAIDS

Rhinegold! Rhinegold!
Purest gold!
How brightly you glowed,
shining so fair on us!
For you, our radiance,
we are mourning.
Give us our gold!
O, give us our radiance again!

LOGE
(looking down in to the valley)

The Rhine-king's children
mourn for their stolen gold!

WOTAN
(who has paused at the bridge)

What mourning rings in my ears!
Accursed nixies!
Stop their harrowing noise!

LOGE
(in das Tal hinabrufend)
Ihr da im Wasser!
was weint ihr herauf?
Hört, was Wotan euch wünscht!
Glänzt nicht mehr
euch Mädchen das Gold,
in der Götter neuem Glanze
sonnt euch selig fortan!
(Die Götter lachen und beschreiten dann die Brücke.)

DIE DREI RHEINTÖCHTER
Rheingold!
Rheingold!
Reines Gold!
O leuchtete noch
in der Tiefe dein laut'rer Tand!
Traulich und treu
ist's nur in der Tiefe:
falsch und feig
ist, was dort oben sich freut!

ENDE

LOGE
(calling down into the valley)
You in the water!
just why do you wail?
Hear what Wotan desires:
nevermore
seek the gleam of the gold!
And instead enjoy the brave new gleam
that comes from the gods!

(The gods laugh and during the following cross the bridge.)

RHINE MAIDS

Rhinegold!
Rhinegold!
Rarest gold!
O may our bright toy
shine again
in the depths of Rhine!
What's in the deep
holds truth and uprightness!
False and weak
is what rejoices above!

THE END